To Noel
Merry Christmas 2018
Love Kimbra + Roger
xx

Argyll

LAND OF BLOOD AND BEAUTY

# Argyll

## LAND OF BLOOD AND BEAUTY

Mary McGrigor

WITH PHOTOGRAPHS BY Gordon Ross Thomson

BIRLINN

To the memory of
Dr F.S. MacKenna, FSA
(1902–97)

*My friend and mentor for many years*

First published in Great Britain in 2000 by
Northabout Publishing, Edinburgh

This edition published in 2013 by
Birlinn Limited
West Newington House
10 Newington Road
Edinburgh
EH9 1QS

*www.birlinn.co.uk*

ISBN: 978 1 78027 071 5

British Library Cataloguing-in-Publication Data
A catalogue record for this book is available from the British Library

Design by Mark Blackadder

Printed and bound by Gutenberg Press, Malta

# Contents

Oban, with McCaig's Tower

# Foreword by His Grace Ian, 12th Duke of Argyll

I can with all sincerity state that when Mary McGrigor, the author of *Argyll: Land of Blood and Beauty*, asked me to write a foreword that I never realised what an awesome task this would be: I am just not equal to adequately attempt to put my overwhelming admiration for this book on paper. The reasons for this are many and varied, one perhaps being that it is so very 'close to home' in every sense of the phrase, as I live in the very centre of all that Mary McGrigor rehearses so vividly with respect to events spanning some 6,000 years, some of which very much affect us even today.

In centuries past, one of the most important and respected members of a family or a clan was the 'Sennachie', a learned man, who would recall the Tales of Heroism or otherwise of the family he served.

He was a veritable encyclopaedia of events past as well as being the in-house poet. To him would be delegated the responsibility of chronicling the major happenings. Now this has been done with the greatest diligence, beauty and all-encompassing passion in this most precious and enlightening book. The remit covers episodes and areas of the county whose name I bear, some of which to my shame I have never even heard about. I strongly recommend *Argyll: Land of Blood and Beauty* to all who have but a passing interest in this historic part of our country as well as those who have a deeper knowledge of the extraordinarily rich heritage that has gone before and are now part-possessors of a proud past which has done so much to mould their being today.

*Argyll*

The Duke of Argyll

## Author's Note

So many people have helped me during the many years which it has taken to research and write this book that it is impossible to name them all. I would like to say a special thank you to: Mrs Adeline Clark; Miss Campbell of Kilberry; Mr Murdo MacDonald (Archivist of Argyll & Bute); Mr Michael Davis (Head of Historical Department, Argyll & Bute Library); Alistair Campbell of Airds (Offical Historian of Clan Campbell); Mr Hugh Andrew of Birlinn Ltd and lastly to my husband and family who have supported me throughout.

Mary McGrigor,
Upper Sonachan, May 2013

## KEY TO MAP OF ARGYLL

1. Achallader Castle
2. Achamore House
3. Achnabreck
4. Achnacloich House
5. Ardchattan Priory
6. Ardtornish Castle
7. Arduaine
8. Aros Castle
9. Barcaldine Castle
10. Barguillean
11. Breacahadh Castle
12. Broch Tirefore Castle
13. Carn Chilean
14. Carnasserie Castle
15. Carrick Castle
16. Castle Lachlan
17. Castle Stalker
18. Castle Suibhine
19. Cill Cholium Chille
20. Craignish Castle
21. Crarae Estate
22. Duart Castle
23. Dunadd
24. Dunaverty
25. Dunollie Castle
26. Dunoon Castle
27. Dunstaffnage Castle
28. Duntrune Castle and Garden
29. Dunyvaig Castle
30. Eilean Mor Chapel
31. Finlaggan Castle

32. Gylen Castle
33. Inch Kenneth Chapel
34. Innis Chonnel Castle
35. Inveraray Castle
36. Iona
37. Kilbrannan Chapel
38. Kilchenzie Church
39. Kilchoman Church
40. Kilchousland Church
41. Kilchurn Castle
42. Kildalton Church
43 Kilkivan Church
44. Kilmarie Church
45. Kilmartin Church
46. Kilmory Knap
47. Kilnave Chapel
48. Kilneuair Church
49. Mingary Castle
50. Moy Castle
51. Nether Largie Cairns
52. Oronsay Priory
53. Saddell Abbey
54. St Charmaig Chapel
55. St Columba's Church
56. St Molnag Cathedral
57. Skipness Castle
58. Stonefield Castle Gardens
59. Tarbert Royal Castle
60. Templewood Stone Circles
61. Toward Castle

CO

TIREE

*ATLANTIC OCEAN*

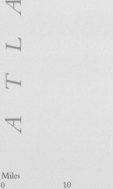

Miles
0                    10                    20

0        10        20        30
Kilometres

©2000 Akeel Ahmad, a4 book design

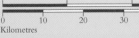

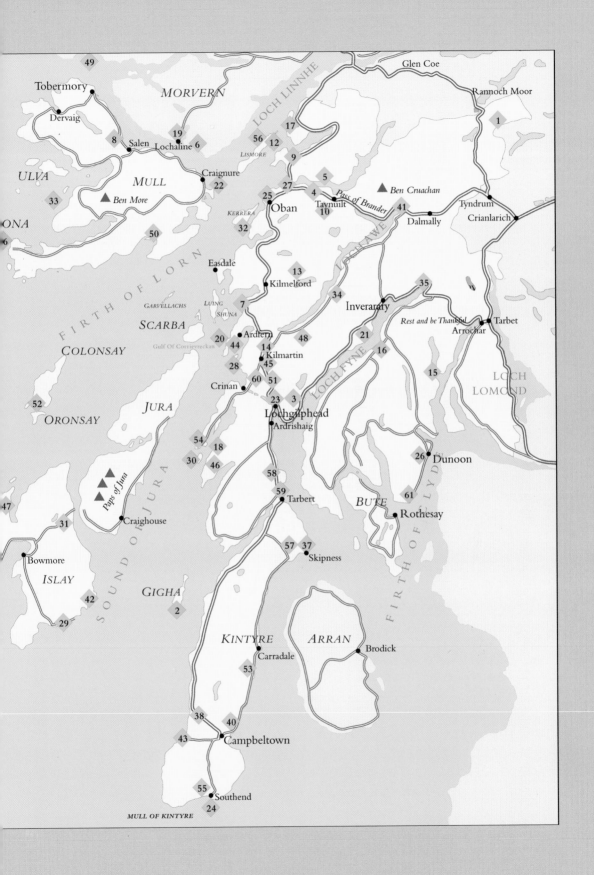

# Introduction

Argyll. Why is it so special? Why does it hold an attraction as insidious as that of the spider who wills its victim gently, and almost imperceptibly, into the toils of its web? Part of its mysterious magnetism may be the element of surprise. Argyll is unpredictable, beautiful beyond comparison in sunshine, savage as a beast in storm. The landscape, like the climate, contrasts vividly to the eye. In the north the mountains of Glencoe seem almost to pierce the sky, while in the south the green fields of Kintyre stretch gently to the ocean's edge.

Always there is water. The coastline of Argyll and the Isles, stretching over 2,800 miles, is longer than that of France. Nowhere can you be more than four miles from either a sea loch or the sea. Travel, until the second half of the 20th century, depended largely on boats. Sailing ships, and later steamers, conveyed people to and from the coasts, while inland a network of ferries were linked to tracks across the land. Only after the building of the military roads, in the latter half of the 18th century, could wheeled vehicles safely be used.

Argyll, like the facets of a cut diamond, changing in differing light, contains both triumph and tragedy within the story of its past. Much of the tale is tortuous, born of a prime need for land. Life, until at least the 18th century, was a struggle for survival. Invaders were brutally massacred, neighbours raided each other, and families, through internecine quarrels, created their own destruction.

Yet even this age of barbarity had its paradox, for artists and masons created outstanding buildings and carvings of exceptional loveliness. The intricate Celtic designs on the group of Iona crosses, which are as early as the 8th century, remain, through the skill of their achievement, an inspiration to behold. Later, in a more peaceful age, the castles of great magnificence were replaced by gracious houses no longer places of defence. Then also came the creation of gardens, where plants from all corners of the earth grow in the mild climate of the west. These are only some of the aspects of a place of ancient habitation dear to the heart of man.

Argyll. Where lies its attraction? What is the secret of its charm?

The answer is largely indefinable. The country has much poor land and the rainfall, particularly in the mountainous areas, remains consistently high. Yet visitors come and return, and people who live here remain. The love of the land is inherent and perhaps this provides an affinity with a place of enduring charm.

## CRUACHAN

Cruachan, the name of the mighty mountain, is synonymous with Argyll. As the rallying cry of Clan Campbell, it refers to the farm of that name on the north side of Loch Awe, opposite the Campbell stronghold of Innis Chonnell – a much more practical gathering place than atop a precipitous ridge. The massive mountain with its seven peaks (the highest being 3,689 ft.), which rises above the north-east end of Loch Awe, is one of the most famous landmarks of the west. The first people who came here, perhaps

OPPOSITE: Ben Cruachan hydro-electric dam

Ben Cruachan from Loch Etive

over 8,000 years ago, probably saw the great massif of the mountain from as far away as Jura. Today, far out over the Atlantic, it is recognisable from the air.

The bones of the land are unchanged despite the activities of man. A large part is made up of rocks belonging to the Dalradian series which were originally mud and sands, largely laid down under the sea. Since their formation about 600,000,000 or more years ago, these rocks have been changed by heat and pressure during the formation of the Caledonian mountain chain, and have become schist, slate, quartzite and limestone. About 400,000,000 years ago these were invaded by large masses of granite, such as that of Cruachan, which were intruded as molten, or partially molten, material and were perhaps capped by volcanoes which have since been largely removed by erosion.

Cruachan is the haunt of the Cailleach, the mythical old woman of whom legends are told the length and breadth of Argyll. The story runs that she was the guardian of a spring of clear water that welled from the highest of Cruachan's seven peaks. She was charged with the duty of covering it with a slab of stone every evening after sundown. But one day, being tired after driving her goats across from Connel, she fell asleep by the side of the spring. It overflowed and the water poured down the mountainside until, with a mighty roar, it broke open an outlet in the Pass of Brander (am Brànradh). The Cailleach woke up with a start but there was nothing she could do to stem the flood which flowed into the plain where all in its path were drowned. Thus was formed Loch Awe

(Loch Odha). The Cailleach, horrified as this happened, turned into a stone. She sits in the Pass of Brander, sinister in shadow, watching the scene of her neglect.

Prior to the last Ice Age, about ten thousand years ago or more, Loch Awe ran out to the west. The river bed can still be traced through the Eurach Gorge from where it continued to the Sound of Jura. Then, as the outlet silted up with sand, melting ice expanded a crack in rocks until pent-up water forced its way through what became the Pass of Brander, from where the River Awe flows four miles northwest to Loch Etive.

Today, in the 21st century, the mountain has a new and vital importance. Work began on the Cruachan Scheme in 1960 when the North of Scotland Hydro-Electric Board built the road up the south side of the mountain to carry men and materials to the site. The squads worked often in appalling weather to construct the massive buttress-type dam above the station. This blocks the mouth of a corrie[1] which was flooded on its completion.

Some hundreds of metres below, deep in the heart of the hill, the giant machine hall houses four reversible turbine generators which draw water from the loch and pump it directly up a vertically rising inclined shaft into the reservoir above. This system, called pump storage, produces around 450,000,000 units of electricity annually. When power is needed on the Scottish grid, the water can be quickly released to surge down the shaft and spin the turbines in a reverse direction so that they can generate electricity.

Cruachan is part of the Awe Scheme which included the nearby Inverawe and Nant Power Stations. It was brought into service in 1963 and completed some two years later. In August 1965 Her Majesty the Queen performed the official opening ceremony and electricity began to flow across the transmission lines to provide light and power for the people of Scotland.

The mountain is a focus for climbers particularly as the main ridge has two peaks, Ben Cruachan and Stob Diamh, both ranked as Munros (over 3,000 ft). The most common climb involves a circuit of Coire Cruachan, with its reservoir. Other routes ascend Meall Cuanall, due south of Ben Cruachan, or from the reservoir to the *bealach* (pass) between Ben Cruachan and Meall Cuanall. The climb is claimed to be steep but easy.

**THE FIRST SETTLERS**

The boy, crouched in the bows of the boat, was the first to see them, the three great peaks of the mountain on the island which seemed to rise from the sea. He gave a cry, pointing ahead with his finger, and the men pulled harder on the paddles, driving the canoe towards the shore. It hit the pebbles with a crunch. The boy leapt over the gunwale, followed by the old dog which sensed familiar surroundings having been here before. They stumbled together up the beach, both of them stiff after the inactivity of many days in the boat. Here was the pile of shells, relics of several years, and here the charred hearthstone, nearly buried by the sand.

One of the older men found the tent poles where he had left them, tied together with a leather thong, behind a sheltering rock. Also there were the deer hides, wrapped in a bundle. Some were partly rotten but, spread over the poles, they would keep most of the rain out until more deer could be killed and their skins scraped clean with stones. They stayed on the island through the long summer nights when it was hardly dark at all. But gradually the days grew shorter and the sun sank lower in the sky. Then one day the wind blew cold from the north and a great flight of birds, with long necks and wings, flew in the shape of an arrowhead towards the south.

The birds were heading for winter quarters, away from the snow-laden storms, and the old men, seeing them, knew it was time to go. From the sea they looked back at the mountains, those three so distinctive peaks, retaining them in their memory for when they would come again. Gradually some of the hunters remained on the west coast of Scotland throughout the whole of the year. They seem to have sheltered in caves throughout the winter months. During the last century workmen laying the foundations of George Street in Oban unearthed remains of their occupation. One cave was found on the site of the present distillery, where visitors can see a reconstruction of the lives of these early settlers.

More recently, in 2012, Dr Clare Ellis of Argyll Archaeology uncovered two ring-ditches and one double post-ring roundhouse at Glenshellach and five ring-ditch roundhouses and one post-ring roundhouse at Dunbeg, dating from the mid Bronze Age, around 1640–1450 BC. The ring-ditches are believed to be some kind of cellarage, which, as early refrigerators, would have had wooden floors. Channels coming from some of the ring-ditches and also from some of the central hearths were a form of underground air ventilation. Other discoveries included several burial pots into which the cremated remains of bodies were placed before being buried in the ground. Another Bronze Age roundhouse has also been found near Killinochonoch Farm in Kilmartin Glen, the first time a domestic settlement of this period has been discovered in the glen. Archaeologists, on the evidence of stone tools and barbed antler points, used as fish spears, have established that they lived largely on molluscs, fish and wild animals, including both deer and boar, which they hunted in the great forests. Circa 4000 BC the first farmers arrived. They brought with them seeds of wheat and barley and a few sheep and cattle, derived from the wild stocks of Asia Minor. They knew how to weave cloth and how to make pottery.

The climate at that time is thought to have been drier than it is today and the evidence of stone axes, discovered below the peat[2], suggests that they cleared

and cultivated the land now covered by the Moine Mhor (the Crinan Moss). Around 2000 BC the 'Beaker People' reached the north-west of Scotland from Europe. They took their name from a distinctive form of pottery, which they placed in the graves of their dead. Some of the earliest examples of Beaker pottery are small, vase-shaped vessels, decorated with an impression of a twisted cord, and in some cases with shells. These people also knew how to work with metal and the copper knives and axes that they used were cast in moulds. The fact that they made bronze, a hard water-resisting alloy compounded of copper and tin, suggests that they travelled to Cornwall where the tin was mined.

Towards the end of the Bronze Age, as this period is called, the climate became much wetter. This was the time when the peat began to grow and the great mosses, like the Crinan Moss and the Moss of Achnacree, on the north side of Loch Etive, were formed.

## THE GLEN OF KILMARTIN

*The Nether Largie Chambered Cairns*

Argyll's greatest concentration of remains of early habitation are found in the Kilmartin area. The former manse in Kilmartin holds artefacts which none who are interested in Scotland's past should miss a chance to see. Kilmartin House Museum is an award-winning organisation dedicated to preserving and interpreting the internationally important landscape of Kilmartin Glen, including the prehistoric ritual landscape and Dunadd, seat of the earliest kings of Scotland.

Some of the finest examples of burial cairns are at Nether Largie, just south of Kilmartin Village. Nether Largie South is a chambered cairn of Neolithic date. The cairn is of the 'Clyde Type', so called because of the great incidence of these graves near to the River Clyde. The chamber at its centre contains four compartments divided by stone slabs. The walls are built largely of dry stone. It was used over and over again for burials, being closed after each until it was finally sealed. In 1864, when the tomb was excavated, finds included a round-based Neolithic vessel, cremated bones, flints, arrowheads, flint implements and the tooth of a cow. Proof that it was used by succeeding generations lies in the remains of Beaker pottery, from the Bronze Age, which have been found there.

The other cairns near to it, known as Nether Largie Mid, and Nether Largie North, which seem to be aligned to it, relate to the Bronze Age. Nether Largie Mid, which stands 400 metres to the north-east of Nether Largie South, was excavated in 1929. It was found to contain two cists. The position of one,

*Standing Stones*[3]

They stand aloof pointing towards the sky.
What is their significance? Who placed them there and why?
Were they symbols of worship, imbued with mysterious rites?
And was there death by sacrifice on still, unhallowed nights?

The full moon rises slowly, casting her light on the land,
And is her passage carved on stone by long forgotten hand?
Cup marks may have shown the date on which to plant the corn,
And old men reckoned carefully the years since they were born.

What is the real meaning of stones erected when
he power of mighty elements controlled the lives of men?
Were they raised as tokens of unknown strength unseen?
And does their present silence embody what has been?

OPPOSITE: The Moine Mhor (Crinan Moss)

Nether Largie South, Kilmartin Glen

whom St Columba of Iona is best known. Excavations have revealed that a chronological sequence exists between them and the other archaeological sites which comprise the greatest concentration of prehistoric monuments in Argyll.

There are in fact two circles – the earliest, the North-east Circle, having been discovered by Mr J.G. Scott during excavations in 1979. This has been reconstructed with concrete markers to indicate the original timber posts (circular markers), which were later replaced by upright stones (rectangular markers). Analysis of a charcoal deposit, found in a socket of stone, has given a radiocarbon date of approximately 3075 BC. This circle is thought to have been taken down in prehistoric times for some reason unknown.

The South-west Circle consists of a ring of standing stones now partly hidden by a surrounding cairn. They were originally twenty-two in number but some have been removed. Two of the cairns, built outside the stone circle, contain burial cists. That on the north-east side was found to contain a beaker, three barbed arrowheads and a flint scraper. The other, on the west side, held the tooth of a child of about five years old. The central cist within the stone circle, built of four enormous stone slabs, contained cremated human remains. During the 19th century the site was surrounded by hand-gathered stones and the trees from which come the name of Temple Wood.

*Achnabreck*

The significance of the mysterious cup-and-ring marks so far remains unexplained. Dating largely from the Bronze Age, they consist of round hollows in stone, pounded and deepened by grinding. Some appear to form a pattern and others are in random form. Theories are legion as to what they represent. The idea that they were early calendars, marking the position of the moon or the sun at certain times, seems possible. Local people may have used them as guides for planting and harvesting.

Some of the best examples in Scotland lie upon sloping rock faces at Achnabreck. The approach is up the old forestry road from the Cairnbaan corner. The site has now been protected by 'viewing bridges' which you can cross to inspect the carvings. The multiple rings and spirals appear to form a design, and the idea of a place of sacrifice rises, involuntarily, to the mind.

which was set in a pit below the cairn, is indicated by concrete posts. The other, which had been dug into the gravel, now stands with its great capstone suspended above it, so that the inside of this long empty coffin can be seen. Nether Largie North stands 150 metres away again to the north-east. During excavations in 1930 it was entirely rebuilt. It was found to contain a massive cist in the centre, in which a human tooth was found, and another enclosing the tooth of an ox and some charcoal.

*The Stone Circles of Templewood*

The stone circles of Templewood stand on the south-west side of the road between Nether Largie and North Lodge Poltalloch, the Chambered Cairn of Nether Largie South being 250 metres to the north-east. Known to be older than both the Pyramids and Stonehenge, they remained of enormous religious significance until the conversion of local people to Christianity by evangelists from Ireland, amongst

Templewood South-west Stone Circle

Cup-and-ring marks at Achnabreck

The broch on Dun Mor Vaul

Broch Tirefore, Lismore

## THE IRON AGE AND EARLY HISTORIC PERIOD (*c*600BC–*c*AD 400)

### The Irish Settlement of Dal Riata (c 500)

Around 700 BC a new race of Celtic people, who came originally from the Danube basin, began to reach western Scotland. They were warriors who reckoned their wealth in cattle and they knew how to work with iron. They also brought with them an art style of intricate design, including foliage and animals, which other craftsmen were to copy throughout succeeding centuries.

The Romans, who invaded Scotland in AD 79, apparently never reached Argyll. The fleet sent north by Agricola to explore the west of Scotland sailed past, but abandoned further exploration in that area, probably because of what the members of the expedition reported. Following the departure of the Romans, however, hostile tribes invaded the land which had been guarded by the Antonine Wall. Foremost amongst them were the Picts, then predominant in the eastern parts of Scotland. Fierce fighting ensued and the local people increasingly relied upon the defence of stone walls. They built forts upon hilltops, which from time immemorial have been natural places of defence. From them a watch can be maintained and assailants targeted on an upward approach. The forts were occupied for centuries, some being dated earlier than the Roman occupation of Britain. They were simply enclosures protected by a single dry-stone wall. In some places, such as Dun Ormidale – a hill overlooking Gallanach to the south-west of Oban – the fort surrounded the whole summit, thus forming a stockade.

Smaller forts, known as duns, seem to have been a later development. Mostly circular in shape, they had massively thick walls. In some cases vitrification of the stone suggests that that they were laced with timber, which, accidentally or intentionally, was set on fire. It is thought that, whereas the larger forts were communal, the duns housed only one, or possibly two, families and possibly adherents as well. A good dun to visit is Druim an Duin, which stands at the north end of a ridge above a sharp bend in the public road (B8025) that runs from the head of Caol Scotnish to Bellanoch. Ruins remain of the massive wall, which contains a guard room beside the entrance on the south-east side. The chamber continues for a short way as an intramural gallery, a feature which aligns it to a broch.

Brochs, which are built of a double wall, with, in most cases, an intramural gallery, are found mostly in the north of Scotland. So far only seven have been discovered in Argyll. All are upon islands, Dun Mor Vaul, in Tiree, and Tirefore Castle in Lismore being the least ruinous and most impressive. Dun nan Gall in Mull, and the broch on the summit of Dun Bhoraraig in Islay, are both much destroyed by stone robbers.

### Crannogs

Crannogs, which are islands constructed of timber and stone, are attributed to this period called the Iron Age, although it is now thought that some may be of earlier date. Certainly they remained as places of refuge until medieval times. Houses, said to have been upon them, were apparently raised on stilts to prevent them being flooded when the level of the water rose. In 1972 a survey by Naval Air-Command Sub Aqua Club found no fewer than twenty crannogs in Loch Awe. Some are below the surface but many can still be seen. The crannog in Cairn Bay, on the eastern side of the loch, contains the logs of its foundation, visible when the level of the loch is low.

In *c*500 AD the Scots of Dal Riata, a small kingdom of Antrim, colonised Argyll. Traditionally the Irish King Erc divided his territory, which he called Dal Riata (or Dal Riada) between his three sons. Fergus received Kintyre and Knapdale and the east side of Loch Fyne. Loarn was given the area around Oban which phonetically bears his name, and Angus got Islay and Jura. Subsequently Fergus divided his patrimony between his grandsons, Comgall, who gave his name to Cowal, and Gabran (ancestor of the Royal family) who received Knapdale. Much communication continued between Dal Riata and the mother country, for many years to come.

### Broch Tirefour Castle – Lismore

Broch Tirefour Castle stands on top of a cliff above the stretch of sea called the Lynn of Lorn on the east coast of the island of Lismore. The building, which is almost circular in shape, surrounds an inner court. The dry-stone walls of great width contain massive boulders in their structure. Traces of an intramural gallery can be seen in places on the inside wall at a height of about 2.7 metres. The broch, both on the north-east and the south-west sides, is protected by outworks of now largely fallen walls.

Compared to other buildings, which date from the same period, the fabric, although in places ruinous, remains remarkably intact. Perhaps it is safe to surmise that, because of its impregnable position and the strength of its defences, it largely withstood attack.

## Dunadd

The Kingdom of Dal Riata (or Dalriada) was centred on the fortress of Dunadd. The ruins stand on an isolated hill, rising above the great sweep of the Moine Mhor, (Crinan Moss) at the mouth of the River Add. Galleys were once rowed upriver to the pool below the stronghold. Perhaps on some of the stretches they may have been poled or even towed.

A steep path leads up the side of the hill to a point where a sheer-sided rocky passage gives entrance to a terrace. Foundations of the buildings, which long ago stood upon it, are now just possible to trace. The ruins of the protective wall, which surrounded them, incorporate the natural rock. Remains of fortifications encircle a small plateau on the summit which was once the site of a fort. Here sentries stood guard, watching for sign of movement both on land and on the seaward approaches to the mouth of the river.

Just below on a rockface, two carved footprints, one barefoot and the other shod, point eastwards towards Cruachan, the great mountain, recognisable by its seven peaks, which lies in the heart of Lorn. In them, according to tradition, the kings of Dal Riata placed their feet while making their vows of office. This was an inauguration ritual taken up by the Lords of the Isles, of which there is a later description. Nearby is a rock-ringed basin. There are also faint vertical scratches, which in fact are lines of Pictish Ogam, but which cannot be translated because the language is unknown.

During the 6th and 7th centuries the Scots kingdom of Dal Riata was invaded by the Picts, from central and eastern Scotland, who attacked with great ferocity. The Annals of Ulster, based on records kept in Iona, state that in AD 736, 'Aengus son of Fergus,

The fortress of Dunadd

Dunadd

King of the Picts, laid waste the territory of Dal Riata and seized Dun At.' The fort is believed to have been occupied for some time after by the Picts. Analysis has shown that repairs were made to the masonry, presumably after times of destruction. The carving of a wild boar, near the footprints, apparently of Pictish origin, may well have been done at this time. Careful scrutiny shows that all the male indications, including tusks and genitalia, have been removed, probably by the Scots when they repossessed the fort.

Traditionally the Stone of Scone, on which Scottish kings were crowned, was first at Dunadd. Taken to Dunstaffnage Castle, it was then carried across to Scone as the threat of invading Norsemen increased.

Dunadd, rising so dramatically from the surrounding moss, is a lasting monument to the Kingdom of Dal Riata. It is one of four fortifications of the original Scots settlers. The others are at Columcille near Southend in Kintyre; Tarbert, on the east coast of Loch Fyne; and Dunollie on the north side of Oban Bay. Dunollie and Columcille were both coronation sites. At Columcille, behind the pre-Reformation chapel which bears Columba's name, a footprint, very similar to that at Dunadd, is incised in a flat rock. Beside it, a second footprint, the work of a local mason, is of 19th-century date.

*Milking Croon*

Come Brendan from the ocean,
Come Ternan, most potent of men,
Come Michael valiant, down,
And propitiate to me the cow of my joy.
Ho my heifer, ho heifer of my love,
Ho my heifer, ho heifer of my love.
My beloved heifer, choice cow of every sheiling,
For the sake of the High King take to thy calf.

Come beloved Colum of the fold,
Come great Bride of the flocks,
Come, fair Mary from the cloud,
And propitiate to me the cow of my love.

The stock-dove will come from the wood,
The tusk will come from the wave,
The fox will come but not with wiles,
To hail my cow of virtues,
Ho my heifer, ho heifer of my love.

From *Carmina Gadelica: Hymns and Incantations*
Translated into English by Alexander Carmichael.

## ST COLUMBA

Shortly after the formation of Dal Riata, at the beginning of the 6th century, missionaries from the great monastic houses of Ireland sailed across to western Scotland.

Circa 540 St Brendan of Clonfert founded churches in Tiree, Bute, Seil, Culbrandan and probably on Eileach nan Naoimh (Island of the Saints) in the Garvellachs. A few years later St Moluag established a religious community on the island of Lismore in Loch Linnhe, and St Kentigern, better known as St Mungo, founded Glasgow Cathedral at about the same time. Then in 563 St Columba, penitent after raising a rebellion against his kinsman the King of Ireland, sentenced himself to banishment beyond sight of his native land. Traditionally he sailed for Scotland with twelve apostles, in a coracle made of hides sealed with tar, stretched over a wooden frame. He is believed to have spent a winter in St Columba's Cave at the head of Loch Caolisport, and to have preached to the local people at Kilcolmkill in Southend, at the southernmost point of Kintyre. Then after returning briefly to Ireland, he once more put to sea to fulfil the self-imposed penance of leaving the country of his birth.

On this second voyage he first went ashore on Colonsay, but finding the shoreline of Ireland still in view, again put out to sea. The little boat passed between dangerous shoals of rock until, almost miraculously, it drifted into the creek known as Port-na-Churach (Port of the Coracle) on Iona. There, from a hilltop, he found to his joy that the faint smudge of land on the horizon had finally disappeared.

Columba made Iona his own. The island was fertile. Cattle would thrive and enough corn could be grown to feed a religious community. Also it had a good anchorage in the channel on the eastern side. The abbot's house of his day was protected by a strong earthen bank. Nearby the patches of cultivated ground were carefully tilled by the monks. Beyond lay the grazing of the machair, the grassland verging on the ocean, rich in the lime of shells.

In summer the ground is carpeted with wild flowers and the air is sweet with the scent of clover and thyme. The sheep and the young cows were herded upon Iona, but the milk cows were kept upon an adjacent island. Women were needed to milk them, and to the saint women meant trouble!

We have it on the authority of Adamnan (c628–704), later abbot of Iona and biographer of the saint, that Columba was a tall man renowned for his commanding presence. Thin to the point of emaciation, because of continual fasting, he slept on a wooden board with his head on a stone pillow. Adamnan, writing of his love of nature, described his strange affinity with living creatures. Once after a storm, he sensed that a crane lay exhausted on a certain place upon the shore. Sending a monk to find it, he nursed

*Incantation by Scandinavian Priests
before a Norse attack upon the Feinne
(from a Tale of Conn, son of Dargo)*

Red mist of Lanno
Dread, astounding.
Striking terror,
Waking horror,
Through the channel
Stream forth our foemen confounding.

Spectre of Odin
Rise before them,
A ghastly wonder;
Clothed in thunder,
From thy Heaven
Shoot forth thine arrowy levin.

Set earth a-quaking.
Storm-floods unsealing,
Loud echoes waking
From mountains pealing,
To flaming skies swift answer making.

Red mist of Lanno
Enwrap, enclose them;
O, mighty Odin
Afflict our foemen,
With nightmare prevent their reposing.

Dread desolator,
Thy fury blight them,
Thy vengeance smite them
Till their soul quailing,
Their spirit failing,
Not one be alive to assail us.

it until it was strong enough to fly on westwards to Ireland.

Later, when he was dying, the old white pony which carried the milk pails from the cow shed to the monastery laid its head upon his bosom and cried like a human being, sensing that his end was near.

St Columba blessed Iona and perhaps his spirit lingers in the place he so greatly loved.

## THE VIKING RAIDS *c*800–1156

The Viking raiders sailed down from Orkney where they had established bases. Their longships with high pointed bows, so instantly recognisable from afar, drew only a few feet of water and could put in on almost any shore. The Norsemen, during the 9th to the 12th centuries, conquered not only the Hebrides and Skye, but much of the north of mainland Scotland. They continued to invade the islands of the west coast, where so many place names denote their occupation, and they steadily encroached upon Argyll.

Lookouts, watching from vantage points, lit fires on sight of the longships to warn of danger to come. The local people, driving their cattle before them, then fled to hiding places in the mountains and deepest woods. The longships, with their lug sails and high prows, were all too easy to recognise, but a story lingers of one instance where watchers were tragically misled. Perhaps the day was misty as what they took to be friendly fishing boats came in towards the shore. Too late, as the wind shifted, they saw light flashing from the metal weather vanes which the longships carried on their masts.

### The Feinne

The Scots of Dal Riata, at the beginning of the Norse attacks, had appealed for help from Ireland and the sagas of Ossian are based upon the Feinne, the legendary warriors, who came in response to the summons.

High above Glen Etive a corrie is known as Deirdre's Bower. Deidre, a girl of exceptional beauty, eloped with her lover Naoise to the fury of the Irish King Conchobar, who wished to marry her himself. With them went Naoise's brothers, taking warriors and hounds. In Glen Etive they lived happily until Conchobar promised forgiveness if they returned.

Deirdre sang her famous 'Farewell to Alba' as the boat pulled away from Scotland's shore. Landing in Ireland Naoise and his brothers were treacherously killed. Deirdre died of sorrow and the lovers are said to be buried beside each other in Armagh.

Finn, who was the leader of the Feinne, was a man of supernatural power, his massive hound Bran being ever by his side. A legend which relates to Dun nan Coin Duibh (Dun of the Black Dogs) near Craobh Haven, tells of how the Norse Prince of Innis Torc came with his champion hound Foir to fight the dogs of the Feinne. Foir finished off 150 of them until, as Bran was unleashed, he was overcome and killed. The dogs are supposed to be buried beneath the mound below the dun.

Finn, according to tradition, had a nephew called Diarmid, whose beautiful wife Grania he himself desired. Diarmid, like Achilles, was impervious to harm, except for a spot on his heel and Finn, in this knowledge, killed a wild boar and then commanded Diarmid to measure it by pacing the length of its body. Diarmid obeyed, a bristle pierced his heel, and Finn refused to save him with healing water from a well.

The site of his death is undetermined. Some claim it to have been in Glen Lonan, where Diarmid's pillar is a standing stone. Others believe it was near Tarbert. In a clearing in Achaglachgach Forest, at the end of a long forestry track, a nine-foot-long oval boulder-surrounded enclosure is claimed to be Diarmid's grave. In Celtic sagas, his galley sailed up the West Loch. Perhaps his spirit still lingers in the mist and the driven spray, for the Feinne believed themselves to be surrounded by the souls of the dead. They also thought that they would hunt after death, in a land to which their souls had risen to the music of harps and the singing of bards.

Somewhere within a Highland cave, the warriors are supposed to lie sleeping, their swords and shields by their sides. A legend tells how a blacksmith, who knew of the hidden place, made a key with which he unlocked the entrance to the cave. There lay the heroes, fast in their swoon of sleep. Each warrior's sword and shield was by his side: the poet's harp close to his hand. Near to the sleeping heroes lay the trumpet which, if blown three times, would awaken the dead as the blacksmith had been told. He blew once and as the cave echoed the warriors blinked their eyes. Twice and they rose on their elbows. The blacksmith, terrified at the sight of them, then fled in terror, throwing away the key. Yet it is said that if Scotland is threatened the Feinne will rise to the call of a trumpet and once again come to her aid.

### The Irish Settlers

During the 11th century, a new wave of Irish settlers arrived with a prince of the O'Neills. He married a local heiress and from them are descended the Cowal clans: MacNeils, Lamonts, MacSweens, MacLachlans, and MacEwens, all of whom became powerful on both sides of Loch Fyne. Many of these families eventually intermarried with people of Norse descent, and Argyll became increasingly dominated by magnates of mixed blood. Despite this fighting continued as new bands of land-hungry Norsemen arrived.

The expedition of Magnus Bareleg, King of Norway, in 1098, resulted in the Scottish King Edgar ceding him all the islands between which a ship could sail. Traditionally Magnus had himself dragged in his

galley across the isthmus between east and west Loch Tarbert, to prove his ownership of Kintyre.

In 1110 a fleet of longships beached on the Otter Spit in Loch Fyne. Apparently there were so many that the men on board could reach the Cowal shore by leaping from one to another across the line of ships. The local people resisted and a battle took place in Glendaruel. The river, so it is said, ran red with blood but the Norsemen were defeated and those who survived the conflict fled back to their ships. Thus the struggle continued until, during the early part of the 12th century, the situation in Argyll became so desperate that many people took refuge in Ireland to escape from constant persecution.

### Somerled

Giolla Bride, Thane of Argyll, believed to have gone to Fermanagh, is said to have raised an army there with which he returned to Scotland in an attempt to regain his territory. He failed. But his son Somerled

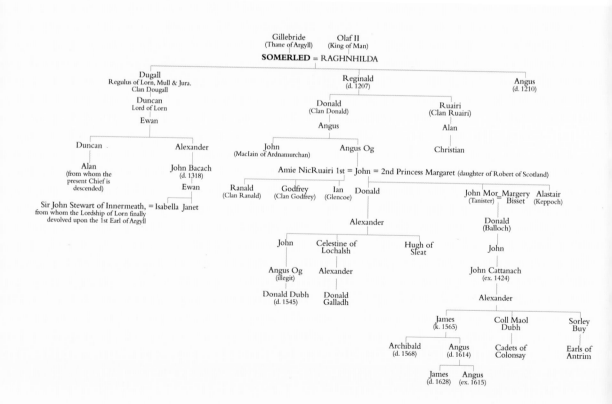

(who probably had a Norse mother) joined him in Morvern, where, according to tradition, they jointly overcame the Norsemen and drove them north of Loch Shiel.

The gradual expulsion of the Scandinavians from the mainland of Scotland continued through the mid-12th century, but their hold on the Hebridean islands was maintained by a monopoly of sea-power. Their longships could not be out-sailed in an open sea but, once within narrow channels they became hard to manoeuvre. Somerled therefore, with great dexterity, designed his own *nyvaigs*, or little ships, which were smaller and easier to handle. Also he fitted them with fighting tops, from which archers could fire down into other vessels, and with hinged rudders, apparently his own invention.

Somerled married the Princess Ragnhilda, daughter of Olaf the Red, King of Norway, with whom he remained on peaceful terms. But Olaf was murdered in 1153 and the son Godred, who succeeded him, proved to be a tyrant. Somerled, approached in his Islay headquarters by the chiefs of the islands, then agreed to their request that his eldest son Dugald should be proclaimed king throughout the isles. But knowing the probable outcome he promptly prepared his *nyvaigs*, which were lying at anchor or beached on the shore in Lagavullin Bay, in the south of the island, in full readiness for war.

Godred, having mustered his galleys, sailed north from the Isle of Man and, on the night of Epiphany, 6 January 1156, the two fleets of warships converged off the north-west coast of Islay. The battle lasted throughout the night until, in the first light of dawn, Godred, finding his fleet destroyed and scattered, finally conceded defeat. By an ensuing treaty he kept only the Isle of Man, while Somerled was acknowledged as overlord of all the Scottish Isles, south of the Treshnish Isles, which lie to the west of Mull.

Somerled strongly resented the policy of David I, who, by granting land to Norman settlers, extended feudal government in Scotland. David was succeeded by his grandson Malcolm IV, who further encouraged the displacement of the old Celtic people from their land. Somerled, intending to confer with Malcolm, on this and other issues, sailed with a large fleet into the estuary of the Clyde. He landed at Greenock, close to Paisley Abbey, where a meeting had been arranged, but prior to its commencement, he was murdered, reputedly at Malcolm's instigation, in his own tent.

Traditionally he is buried at Saddell Abbey, which he himself may have founded, in the beautiful south-facing glen on the east coast of Kintyre. Today he is remembered, not only as the champion of his people, but also for his opposition to the thralldom of a form of ruling he abhorred.

Castle Suibhne, Knapdale

Skipness Castle, Knapdale

## CHAPTER 2

The Lords of Argyll and the Isles

*Descendants of Somerled*

Somerled left his lands to his sons in the form of Celtic Principalities. The eldest, Dugall, progenitor of Clan MacDougall, became king or lord of Ergadia (north and mid Argyll) and of the adjacent islands including Mull, Tiree, Coll and Lismore. Subsequently his descendants became the Lords of Lorn.

The second son, Reginald, or Ranald, inherited the islands of Islay, Jura and Colonsay, and Kintyre on the mainland. A third son, Angus, came into Bute and part of Arran and the area known as Garmoran (Ardnamurchan to Glenelg). But he was then killed, and his territory eventually went through marriage to the MacDonalds of the Isles and Kintyre.

*Builders of Mighty Fortresses*

Today, almost 800 years after they lived, the immediate descendants of Somerled and their vassals are remembered as the builders of the mighty strongholds, sited in strategic positions on the coasts and inland waterways throughout their widespread domains.

The influence of continental forms of architecture, introduced by Norman invaders during the 11th century, emerges in the massive curtain walls, designed to protect the square towers and domestic offices within. Also the use of lime, which consolidated the stones of walls, built double and filled with loose rubble, made these buildings virtually impregnable to the weapons of medieval times.

Transport not only in the islands but also in mainland Argyll, with its long coastline and many rivers and lochs, was, until fairly recent times, almost exclusively by boat. A glance at the map shows how castles were sited by waterways, in many cases on opposite shores so that messages could be flashed across by lights. Warnings could be transmitted from Mull and Morvern to Dunollie Castle above Oban, through the chain of fortresses built by the MacDougalls of Lorn, on strategic positions, both east and west of the Sound of Mull.

*The Castles of the MacDonalds of Islay and Kintyre*

Castle Suibhne, Knapdale

Reputedly the oldest stone-built castle in Argyll, this is an outstanding example of the architecture brought to Scotland by the Normans. Standing upon low cliffs, on the eastern shore of Loch Sween in Knapdale, it was placed to give protection from invasion from the sea. It is believed to have been built by one of the family of Suibhne, or Sween, who came in the 11th century from Ireland with a prince of the O'Neills.

The main block, the oldest part of the castle dating from the 12th century, with its arched doors and flat buttresses, stands within a curtain wall. Inside the courtyard is a well, of utmost importance in a time of siege. Below the castle there was once a sea-gate, but this at some time has been blocked.

Following the Treaty of Perth in 1266[4], in the second half of the 13th century, the MacSuibhnes (or MacSweens) lost their lands in Knapdale to the Stewart Earls of Menteith.[5] Then in 1376 King Robert II granted half of the area, including Castle Suibhne, to his son-in-law John, Lord of the Isles. The MacNeills of Gigha became hereditary captains of the castle for the Lords of the Isles. They were succeeded by MacMillans and the 'MacMillan Tower' was added to the north-east end during the 15th century. In 1481 the castle was granted by James III to the 1st Earl of Argyll. In 1615 it was garrisoned by the 7th Earl when Sir James MacDonald of Islay raised a rebellion in an attempt to reclaim his ancestral lands in Islay and Kintyre. In 1647 it was seized and burned by Alasdair MacColla, lieutenant of Montrose during the Civil War.[6] Thereafter it remained uninhabited.

## Skipness Castle, Kintyre

Standing a short way above the shore of Skipness Bay, the castle was placed there to guard the confluence of Kilbrannan Sound, Loch Fyne and the Sound of Bute. The castle was built in the first half of the 13th century,

Castle Dunyvaig, Islay

again by one of the MacSweens. A document of 1261, which mentions both a tower-house and a chapel, shows that it was held by Dugald, son of Sween, for the MacDonald lords of Islay and Kintyre. In 1262 it passed to Walter Stewart, Earl of Menteith.

It was rebuilt *c*1306, probably on the instigation of Edward I of England, with whom the MacDonalds were then briefly in alliance, to resist the threat of the MacDougalls of Lorn who then opposed him. The castle was enlarged and surrounded by a high curtain wall of stone and lime. The earlier hall-house was incorporated and a new chapel built to the south-east near the sea.

Following the forfeiture of the Lord of the Isles in 1493, the castle was granted by the crown to the 2nd Earl of Argyll.[7] Besieged unsuccessfully by the MacDonalds in 1646–7, it shortly after became uninhabited. It is now in the care of Historic Scotland.

## The Castle of Dunyvaig, Islay

The castle of Dunyvaig, attributed to Donald, progenitor of Clan Donald (1207–1249) was built specifically to guard Lagavulin Bay, on the south coast of Islay. The ruined fortress stands like a sentinel above the natural harbour where once the fleet of Somerled's *nyvaigs* lay in readiness for war. Reconstruction was carried out during the 16th century and the use of the natural rock to strengthen the fortification is a particular feature of the building.

The castle's importance as a fortress resulted in it being a key factor in the struggle between the MacDonalds and the Crown, from which Islay was bought in the 17th century by the Campbells of Calder.

## The Castle of Mingary, Ardnamurchan

Mingary, standing on a promontory of rock above the entrance to Loch Sunart, dates from the mid-13th century. It was probably built by a descendant of Reginald, son of Somerled, to defend the important sea passage of the Sound of Mull. A massive curtain wall contains three ranges of buildings, and a stair in the north-west corner of the courtyard leads to the parapet walk. Boats can land below the castle at most stages of the tide. A path cut in the rock leads up to the main north-west entrance, and a sea-gate, later inserted in the south curtain wall, gave easier access to the shore.

Castle Mingary, Ardnamurchan

In 1309, following his conquest of Argyll, Robert the Bruce granted Ardnamurchan to Angus, Lord of the Isles, who bequeathed it to his younger brother, Iain Sprangach (the Bold) progenitor of the MacIains of Ardnamurchan. The castle was burned twice in the early 16th century by Sir Donald MacDonald of Lochalsh in revenge for the capture of John Catanach of Dunyvaig and his sons by MacIain, and their subsequent execution by King James IV[8]. In 1588, when a galleon of the Spanish Armada took refuge in Tobermory Bay in Mull, Lachlan MacLean, chief of the MacLeans of Duart, provisioned her in return for the loan of a hundred soldiers with whom he laid siege to Mingary.

In 1520, Colin, 3rd Earl of Argyll, obtained the superiority of Ardnamurchan. The MacLeans remained in occupation, but in 1612, the 6th Earl granted a commission to Sir Donald Campbell of Barbreck Lochawe, to occupy Mingary. The MacLeans, rising in rebellion, were defeated, and Sir Donald then received the whole of Ardnamurchan. Mingary was captured by Alastair MacColla MacDonald, lieutenant of Montrose, in 1644, but was re-taken by General David Leslie in 1647. The rebuilding of the wall-head defences of the north-west part of the curtain wall probably date from this time.[9]

Sir Donald Campbell died in 1651 and in 1696 the estate of Ardnamurchan was granted by the 10th Earl of Argyll to the Campbells of Lochnell, who are thought to have built the north range of buildings in the courtyard. In 1723, it was bought by Alexander Murray of Stanhope, who died in 1743. Two years later, in 1745, Donald Campbell of Auchindoun, factor of Ardnamurchan to the 3rd Duke of Argyll, then living at Mingary, sent news that Prince Charles had landed at Moidart. The castle was then garrisoned and the soldiers took part in destroying the property of Jacobites in Morvern.

In c1777 Ardnamurchan estate was bought by Mr James Riddell, whose descendants remained there until 1848. Some building was done within the courtyard during the 18th century, and the castle is known to have been at least partly inhabited as late as 1838.

Ardtornish Castle, Morvern

Ardtornish was built either by the MacRuairi Lords of Garmoran or by the MacDonalds of the Isles in

Dunaverty

the late 13th century. Standing high on a cliff, on the south-east side of Loch Aline, it commanded the whole of the eastern section of the vitally important shipping lane of the Sound of Mull. Following the amalgamation of the Earldom of Ross with the Lordship of the Iles[10], Ardtornish, because of its central position, became a convenient assembly point for the Lordship of the Isles.[11]

After the forfeiture of the Lordship of the Isles in 1494, Ardtornish was granted to the MacLeans of Duart. The MacLeans of Ardtornish were baillies in Morvern for their chief of Duart in the late 16th century. Following the acquisition of the MacLean of Duart estates by the 9th Earl of Argyll in 1674[12], the castle was left unoccupied. It then became largely ruined but some restoration was done in 1873 and in the 20th century.

## The Royal Castle of Tarbert, Kintyre

The plateau above steeply rising ground at the entrance of the harbour of Tarbert has been the site of a fortification from very early times. The Annals of Ulster record an ancient fort, destroyed in AD 712 by Sellbach, King of Dal Riata, and again in 731 by Dugald the Violent, his son. During the 13th century a castle was built either by the MacDonalds of the Isles or by

Alexander II or Alexander III. It must have been a formidable structure, for the ruins of the Inner Bailey, built round an open courtyard, consist of four ranges of buildings, designed to hold a large garrison.

Tarbert was already a royal castle when granted by John Balliol (1292–96) to Edward I of England. Robert the Bruce captured it in 1309 during his campaign in Argyll. Later he enlarged and strengthened the building with the addition of the curtain wall, which, containing the two drum towers and the gatehouse, encloses nearly two acres.

In the spring of 1494 King James IV, who on the forfeiture of John Lord of the Isles had just acquired the Lordship, determined to show his authority by making a voyage to Kintyre. Landing at Tarbert, he realised the pivotal importance of the castle. In 1504 Archibald, 2nd Earl of Argyll, was made Hereditary Governor of Tarbert Castle by James IV.[13] Subsequently, after both the King and Argyll had died in the battle of Flodden, in 1513, the castle was seized by Alan MacDonald of Islay who let it be held by a pirate named Alan nan Sop. Sentries on the parapet watched for sign of a sail. Ships were seized in Loch Fyne. Then Alan, getting bolder, raided as far as the Scottish Lowlands and across the Irish Sea. Undefeated, he terrorised the district from his hide-out until, at an old age, he died in 1555.

Almost a hundred years later Tarbert Castle was garrisoned by Cromwell's men with the acquiescence of the Marquess of Argyll. The soldiers, however, grew negligent and local men seized the castle and purloined most of the stores and ammunition while the soldiers were out gathering nuts. In 1685 Tarbert was the assembly point for the forces of the 9th Earl of Argyll when he joined the Duke of Monmouth in an attempt to overthrow James VII & II[14]. During the late 17th and early 18th centuries a local family of MacAlisgers were tenants, but upon their building a new house, the castle was left unoccupied and became a ruin.

On 6 September 1974 a ceremony took place in Tarbert when the Colonel of the Argyll and Sutherland Highlanders was appointed Captain of the Castle with a magnificent golden key, handed over to each succeeding holder of the post. In 1990 the Tarbert Castle Trust was formed by a group of local people who launched an appeal for funds towards the restoration of one of the most historically important castles in Argyll. The castle is now owned by Tarbert and Skipness Community Trust, who, with the volunteer organisation Tarbert Conservation Initiative, have opened up the site, secured the ruins and improved visitor access.

## Dunaverty Castle

This once strong castle of the MacDonalds was sited on the southern tip of Kintyre on a headland jutting into the Sound of Sanda between Dunaverty Bay and Brunerican Bay. A natural stronghold, surrounded on three sides by the sea, it is linked to the mainland by a narrow path. It was here, in the summer of 1494, that King James IV on his voyage to Kintyre, having left the castle of Tarbert, came ashore. Aware of the castle's importance he installed a governor to control the surrounding district so lately in possession of the forfeited Lord of the Isles.

Having done so he went aboard his ship but, while still in sight of the castle, looked back to see his newly appointed custodian being hanged by marauding MacDonalds over the castle walls. Because of its rocky prominence Dunaverty did not have a well. Depending, as it did, on a piped water supply from the mainland, it was to prove vulnerable when besieged. The tragic story of this happening will be found in a later section of this book.

## The Castles of Cowal

### Dunoon Castle

The castle, which dates from the first half of the 13th century, was situated on a promontory to protect a main waterway across the Firth of Clyde. Originally a royal castle, it was captured by an English force, in support of Edward Balliol, during the reign of King David II in 1334.[15] Retaken by the Steward of Scotland with the help of Sir Colin Campbell of Lochawe (who became Hereditary Governor) the castle belonged to the Steward when, as Robert II, he became King of Scotland in 1371.

Mary Queen of Scots stayed in the castle when she came to Argyll in July 1563.[16] The building was abandoned as a residence in the mid-17th century, when many of the stones were taken for another use. Nonetheless it retained historical significance. Queen Elizabeth II visited Dunoon in 1958 and was presented with a single rose by the Captain of Dunstaffnage, acting for the Duke of Argyll, in token of the hereditary office of Governor of the Castle, bestowed upon his ancestor Sir Colin Campbell in 1374.

### Toward Castle

The ruins of Toward Castle stand in the grounds of the Victorian mansion of Castle Toward, on the north shore of the Clyde Estuary, some seven miles south of Dunoon. The castle, a three-storey tower house, was built at one end of a rectangular court yard, c1470, by the Lamonts, a clan descended from Irish settlers of the 12th century. By the 14th century, the chiefs were entitled of Inveryne, a place on their land near Kilfinnan. The courtyard is entered through an arch displaying a double roll-and-hollow moulding of great artistic beauty, probably of late-16th century date. The west wall was strongly fortified but the east wall, with a single range of buildings, proved fatally vulnerable to attack.

Mary, Queen of Scots was entertained by Sir John Lamont at Toward Castle when she came to Argyll in 1563. In May 1646, a strong force commanded by Campbell of Ardkinglas came in by ship from Ayrshire to land below Toward. Nine cannons, trained on the castle, began a heavy bombardment. The unfortified east range was badly holed and people within it killed. Sir James Lamont then agreed to surrender

Toward Castle, Cowal

both Toward and his fortress of Asgog near Loch Fyne, on honourable terms. Men from both garrisons were held in Toward until taken by boat to a court martial, held within the kirk of Dunoon.

On Sunday 14 June 1646 they were executed, actually within the churchyard, by enemies insensible with fury. Over a hundred were shot or dirked, while their leaders, cadets of Clan Lamont and their tenants, 36 in all, were first hanged from a tree and then cut down and buried alive. Later when the tree was cut down the roots were said to spout blood. Sir James Lamont and his brother Archibald were taken to Inveraray and survived imprisonment in irons. But his wife and five little children, three of whom died of starvation, were left to live off whatever they could find on the shore. Sir James's estates were restored to him in 1661, but he never again lived at Toward Castle, which gradually fell to ruin.

The now long derelict Ascog Castle, probably of 14th-century date, was another stronghold of the Lamonts in Cowal.

## Castle Lachlan, Cowal

The imposing ruin of Castle Lachlan stands on a promontory above Loch Lachlan, an inlet on the east side of Loch Fyne. Dating from the 15th century it was built, apparently on the site of an older castle, as a stronghold of the MacLachlans, a clan descended from Lachlan Mor, great-grandson of the common ancestor of the Lamonts, MacLachlans and Mac-Sweens, then predominant on both sides of Loch Fyne. The plan of the building greatly resembles that of Castle Sween, two main ranges of four storeys, and a small north-west wing being connected within the massive curtain wall.

In 1745, Lachlan MacLachlan of MacLachlan called out his men for Prince Charles, son of the Jacobite claimant to the throne. MacLachlan asked Archibald, 3rd Duke of Argyll, for a safe conduct to join the Prince. This was granted, but for the outward journey only. Forthwith, ferried in flat boats across Loch Fyne, MacLachlan with his men landed on the opposite shore. But, as he raised his standard, the flag flew widdershins (anti-clockwise) around the pole. There were cries of dismay for this was a bad omen. This was proved when Lachlan was killed by a cannon-ball at the battle of Culloden on 16 April 1746. Miraculously, however, guided by the incredible memory for direction which horses are known to possess, his sorrel mare found her way home to Argyll. Swimming across the loch she reached her own stable, close to the castle walls. Her story thus ended happily but afterwards a ghostly lady was seen standing on the point gazing across the loch for the soldier who would never return.

Following the Rising, on the order of the Duke of Argyll, the castle was bombarded and damaged from the sea. Shortly afterwards it was abandoned and the MacLachlans built the house nearby where Mr Ewan MacLachlan of MacLachlan, 25th chief of his clan, lives today.

## Carrick Castle, Loch Goil

The gaunt rectangular tower of Carrick Castle was built as a garrison on the west coast of Loch Goil (an inlet of Loch Long) by the Campbells of Loch Awe, probably in the late 14th century. Access was mainly by sea, but the castle was entered by a drawbridge on the landward side.

Mary Queen of Scots stayed here before reaching Inveraray in 1563. The castle was burned by government forces in 1685, when the 9th Earl of Argyll was attainted following his rising with the Duke of Monmouth against James VII & II in that year.

### The Castles of the MacDougall Lords of Argyll

### Dunollie Castle, Lorn

A castle of Dunollie, known to have been a chief stronghold of the kings of Dalriada, is recorded early in the 8th century. Standing upon a cliff top above the north end of Oban Bay, it commands a panoramic view of the Firth of Lorn and the distant island of Mull. Dunollie is thought to be one of the three castles mentioned by John Bacach (son of Alexander of Argyll) in his appeal to Edward II for help against King Robert the Bruce.[17]

The lordship of Lorn and the islands held by Alexander of Lorn were forfeited after his surrender to Bruce (see p. 34). The MacDougalls, however, like so many families in times of civil war, were divided in loyalty to the opposing sides. Alexander of Argyll's younger brother Duncan fought for both William Wallace and Robert the Bruce, and in 1310 he was recognised as the 6th chief of the clan. Shortly afterwards Dunollie was granted to Sir Arthur Campbell,

Dunollie Castle, overlooking the Firth of Lorne, outside Oban

cousin of Bruce's supporter Sir Neil, but the fact that Duncan MacDougall remained styled 'of Dunollie' suggests that he may have exchanged the castle for another fortress. John Bacach's son Ewan, who was restored as Lord of Lorn between 1330 and 1335, became the 7th chief, but the chiefship returned to Duncan's grandson Iain in the following generation. In 1388 the estates of the MacDougalls passed through marriage to the Stewarts of Innermenath. But in 1451 John Stewart of Lorn made a grant of Dunollie to John MacDougall, descendant of the MacDougall Lords of Lorn, who was probably the builder of the ruined castle of today.

A tower house of four storeys, to which later additions have been made, stands in the north-east end of the courtyard which is enclosed by a curtain wall.

In c1470, when Colin, 1st Earl of Argyll, again through marriage, acquired the Lordship of Lorn, Dunollie remained with the MacDougalls, who still held the bailery of Lorn. Years later, c1747, Alexander MacDougall, 23rd of Dunollie, abandoned the old castle in favour of the more comfortable house, below the castle, which remains the home of his descendants. Dunollie houses a museum and the renowned Hope MacDougall collection, and is open each year from 23 March – November.

## Dunstaffnage Castle

Dunstaffnage, designed to protect the entrance to Loch Etive, remains the most imposing of the castles of Argyll. The earliest part of the building, dating from the mid-13th century, may have been begun by Duncan MacDougall, known as Duncan of Argyll, who died in 1247. Duncan's son Ewan (d. 1265) probably achieved its completion.

A massive curtain wall encircles the summit of the rock which forms the castle's foundation. A parapet-walk around it, connecting through the upper floors of two angle towers, was constantly patrolled by sentries keeping ever-vigilant watch. Blocks of two-storeyed buildings, on the north-east and west sides of the courtyard, housed the chief with his family and retainers. Dunstaffnage was surrendered by Alexander of Argyll to King Robert the Bruce in 1308. Alexander's lands were forfeited, and Sir Arthur Campbell of Loch Awe became the king's custodian of the castle. John Bacach's son Ewan, however, was restored

as the Lord of Lorn, possibly because he married Lady Matilda Bruce. Their two daughters shared the inheritance, there being no male heir. The daughters married brothers, Sir John and Sir Robert Stewart of Innermeath and Durrisdeer. The latter then exchanged his wife's part of the Lordship for the whole of Durrisdeer.

For the next three generations Dunstaffnage remained the headquarters of the Stewart Lords of Lorn. But history repeated itself when John Stewart, grandson of the earlier John, again had only daughters, this time three girls. The eldest married Colin, Lord Campbell, later to become first Earl of Argyll, who saw to it that her sisters married Campbells, thereby, as he thought, bringing into his hands the still large area of the Lordship, stretching from Ballachulish, at the mouth of Loch Leven, to Kilmartin.

But John Stewart had a natural son called Dougall by a woman of the MacLarens whom he planned to marry, thereby legitimizing their child. Colin Campbell, told of this, determined to prevent it happening. He hired a reprobate called Alan MacCoull, who, with a gang of cut-throats, set about John Stewart as he walked from the castle to the chapel where the wedding was to take place. Overcome by the Stewarts, MacCoull made off, believing he had left John for dead. But carried into the chapel he managed to whisper the vows of marriage with his dying breath.

Dougall, although apparently the rightful heir, was deprived of his inheritance by his uncle Walter Stewart, who, to gain his own ends, may even have been involved in his brother's murder. Then in April 1470 after a complicated financial agreement, Walter finally resigned his lands to the King, who in turn gave a Royal Charter of the Lordship of Lorn to Colin, Earl of Argyll. Subsequently, however, although the greater part of Lorn was under the suzerainty of Argyll, the Stewarts retained Appin where their descendants remain to this day.

During the 16th and 17th centuries Dunstaffnage, held by hereditary Captains, remained one of the most important garrisons on the north-west coast of Scotland. During the civil war c1644, Coll Ciotach MacDonald, father of Montrose's lieutenant, Alasdair MacColla MacDonald, was held prisoner in the castle and is said to be buried below the steps of the chapel which stands nearby.[18]

Repairs and alterations continued throughout the 17th century, and a new two-storeyed house, at

Dunstaffnage Castle

the end of the north-west block, was built by the Captain of Dunstaffnage in 1725. Flora MacDonald stayed here in 1746.[19] In 1962 the greater part of the castle was entrusted to the Department of Environment which carried out extensive repairs. It is now administered by Historic Scotland.

## Duntrune Castle, Mid Argyll

The original castle of Duntrune, placed on a rocky eminence on the north shore of Crinan Loch to guard the harbour below, is believed to have been built by Ewan, Lord of Lorn, who died in 1265. Following the defeat of his descendants by King Robert the Bruce, it was granted as part of the Lordship of Ardskeodnish to the Campbells of Loch Awe. Following this the northern part of the land, known as the Poltalloch estate, was feued by the Campbells to the MacCallums in 1562. The L-shaped tower house of the existing castle, dating from about 1600, stands within a courtyard of roughly octagonal shape. Two ranges of modern buildings, constructed of much similar stone, are also within the walls.

Famous amongst legends is that of the piper, sent by the MacDonalds to see if the castle could be taken by assault. Having somehow gained entry, he realised that this was impossible due to the narrowness of the stair. The Campbell garrison, somehow guessing at his identity, then imprisoned him in a turret. Hiding around the castle they waited to spring an attack. Through a crack of a window in the turret the piper could just see the MacDonald galleys sail into Crinan Bay. Aware of their danger he played a pibroch on his pipes, which was recognised by a piper on one of the galleys as a warning in the secret code of MacCrimmon. The galleys put about and the Campbells, seeing this happen, killed the piper, having first cut off the fingers which, by playing the pibroch, had given their plan away. Afterwards, on still nights, the piper was heard playing round the castle walls. Then, in the 19th century, when repairs were being carried out, a skeleton without fingers was found in a niche in a wall.

In 1615 the forces of the 7th Earl of Argyll assembled at Duntrune, prior to his defeat of Sir James MacDonald of Dunyvaig. Later, in 1646, during the Civil War between Charles I and the government, Duntrune was amongst the castles which the Marquess of Argyll provisioned with meal. In 1796 Duntrune was bought by the Malcolms of Poltalloch, whose fortunes had been founded in Jamaica. They lived there for about fifty years until, as the castle became too small, they built the now roofless mansion of Poltalloch House.

Following the Second World War, between 1954–57, Colonel and Mrs George Malcolm rebuilt and modernised Duntrune and made it their permanent

Duntrune Castle

Duart Castle, Mull

home. His son Mr Robin Malcolm, 19th chief of his clan, now lives there with his family. The castle is not open to the public.

## Duart Castle, Mull

Duart, standing on a peninsula on the south-east coast of Mull seems, even today, to dominate the surrounding seas. Built in the 13th century, it is believed to have been one of the key fortresses placed by the MacDougall Lords of Lorn above the Sound of Mull.

Following the defeat of the MacDougalls by King Robert the Bruce in 1308, Mull was amongst the islands granted to Angus MacDonald of Islay and Kintyre. In 1367 his grand-daughter married MacLean of Duart. The Papal Dispensation which allowed the marriage of Lachlan Lubanach MacLean to Mary, daughter of John, Lord of the Isles, is the first record of the family. Lachlan almost certainly built the tower house within the earlier curtain wall. The difficulty of the confined space was overcome by the placing of massive buttresses against the outside walls. The south-east section was also rebuilt with apertures for weaponry through which guns could be trained. During the early 1600s the MacLeans refurbished and enlarged the castle. The date 1633 is inscribed over the inner doorway along with the initials S.L.M. (Sir Lachlan Maclean).

Following the civil war between Charles I and the parliamentarians (1642–46) the MacLeans were amongst the families who suffered for their loyalty to the Crown. Sir Allan MacLean of Duart was heavily in arrears, and in 1674 the 9th Earl of Argyll offered to buy up his debts. Sir Allan died shortly afterwards and Argyll seized and garrisoned Duart. The MacLeans, aided by the MacDonalds of Glengarry, rose in defiance. Argyll sent his brother, Lord Neil Campbell, with a naval force to subdue them, but the ships were scattered in a storm, believed to have been raised by a witch. The case, however, then went before the Privy Council, which decided in favour of Argyll and subsequently the lands of the MacLeans of Duart in Mull passed into his possession.

The estates were returned to the MacLeans of Duart in 1681, but in 1685, when Sir John MacLean of Duart supported the Jacobites, his castle was bombarded by English warships. In 1681 the MacLeans were defeated in the battle of Cairnburg and their estates were forfeited to the Crown. Duart was then garrisoned by government troops until 1751, when the roof was taken off and the castle was abandoned.

In 1911, the now ruined castle was bought by Sir Fitzroy MacLean, 25th of Duart, from its then owners the Murray Guthries. Sir Fitzroy then immediately commissioned the Glasgow architect, Sir John Burnet, to restore and rebuild the castle and added the beautiful Sea Room with its views of the Sound of Mull. The castle, which is open to the public, is now the home of Sir Lachlan Maclean Bt., 18th chief of Clan MacLean.

## Aros Castle, Mull

The now ruined castle, about 2 km north-west of the village of Salen, was once the most important link with the mainland on the island of Mull. Attributed to Ewan of MacDougall, Lord of Argyll, who died in 1265, it was built upon a promontory at the north of the Aros River to protect both the narrow isthmus across the island and the central stretch of the Sound of Mull. Messages flashed by lights were sent to and received from Ardtornish Castle on the east shore of the Sound.

King Robert the Bruce, after his defeat of the MacDougalls in 1308, awarded Mull to the MacDonalds of Islay and Kintyre and during the 15th century Aros became a main residence of the Lords of the Isles. Following the forfeiture of John, in 1493, the castle came into the possession of the MacLeans of Duart. In 1608 Lord Ochiltree, the King's lieutenant, summoned the chiefs of the Southern Isles to attend a court at Aros.[20]

Aros was part of the Duart properties acquired by the 9th Earl of Argyll in 1674. The castle is said to have been garrisoned by the Campbells in 1690, but thereafter abandoned, it fell into a ruined state.

## Moy Castle, Mull

The castle stands at the head of Loch Buie, about 10 miles south-west of Craignure. One of the best examples of a 15th-century tower house, of three storeys and a garret, much of the shell remains almost intact to the wall head, which is surrounded by a parapet walk. It is believed to have been built by Hector, brother of Lachlan MacLean of Duart, who acquired the land of Lochbuie from the Lord of the Isles in the late 14th century. A legend tells how a MacLean of

Duart, wishing to obtain the property, imprisoned his kinsman of Lochbuie on the Treshnish island of Cairnburg. His only companion, an ugly old woman, thought to be long past child-bearing, however produced a child. Lochbuie himself was murdered, but the woman escaped with her son who managed to regain his estate.

MacLaine of Lochbuie opposed the Revolution Settlement of 1690, which followed the accession of William and Mary, and was forced to surrender to the 10th Earl of Argyll, who installed a garrison within the castle. The MacLaines left Moy Castle in 1752 in favour of a more comfortable house nearby. The castle, left empty, became a ruin. But the ghost of a headless horseman, said to be that of Ewan MacLaine who was slain in battle, reputedly haunts his ancient home.

## Breachachadh Castle, Coll

The island of Coll in the 13th century was held by the MacDougall Lords of Lorn, but following their defeat by King Robert the Bruce, in 1308, it was included in the grants of land which the King gave to Angus MacDonald of Islay and Kintyre.

Circa 1430, Coll was granted by his descendant, Alexander Lord of the Isles, to John Garbh, son of MacLean of Duart, and ancestor of the MacLeans of Coll. Breachachadh Castle, standing at the head of an inlet on the south-west shore of the island, is believed to have been built by him to guard against approach from the sea. The original tower house of four storeys contained a staircase within the south wall, which rose to the parapet walls. The east and the south sides of the tower were protected by a curtain wall against which a hall and other buildings were later constructed.

In 1578, when the MacLeans of Coll were fighting with the MacLeans of Duart, Breachachadh Castle was captured and garrisoned by Lachlan MacLean of Duart. Following their repossession of the castle c1588, the MacLeans of Coll rebuilt part of the tower house and heightened the curtain wall. On the death of Hector Maclean, 6th of Coll, in 1593, the MacLeans of Duart again seized Breachachadh with the intention of pulling it down. Fortunately they failed to achieve this but, following their departure, in 1596, the upper part of the tower house had to be rebuilt and an artillery battery was constructed on the north side to defend the landward approach. During the late 17th century a house, three storeys high, was built within the courtyard on the foundations of the early hall. But despite these extensive alterations the castle was abandoned as a dwelling house and left to decay c1750.

In 1856 John Lorne Stewart, chamberlain of the Argyll Estates in Kintyre, bought Coll from the MacLeans. The old castle of Breachachadh, by then entirely ruined, was sold by Mr Kenneth Stewart to Major Nicholas MacLean Bristol in 1967.[21]

## Gylen Castle, Kerrera

Gylen Castle on the south-west tip of Kerrera, standing upon rocks too dangerous for a ship to approach, was probably built by Duncan MacDougall of MacDougall and Dunollie in 1582. The Gaelic word *geimhlean* means fountains and two freshwater springs lie close beside the castle.

In 1647 the MacDougalls, as Royalists, were suppressed by General David Leslie, who ordered the execution of the garrison and the destruction of the castle by fire. Following the destruction it was found that the Brooch of Lorn, kept at Gylen for safety, had disappeared. It remained lost until, in 1819, Major Campbell of Bragleen died. His trustees found a brooch at the bottom of his Charter Chest, together with an old piece of brown paper on which faint writing confirmed that it was indeed the long-lost Brooch of Lorn. Gylen Castle, never re-occupied, remains spectacular in isolation. Currently the MacDougall family, concerned about the castle's decay, have organised repairs. In May 2006 a restoration of the castle was completed with a £300,000 grant by Historic Scotland and £200,000 raised by worldwide members of Clan MacDougall.

## Defeat of King Haakon of Norway

During the 13th and 14th centuries the MacDougall Lords of Lorn and the chiefs of the MacDonalds of the Isles, although nominally acknowledging the suzerainty of the Kings of Scotland, were virtually independent rulers.

The MacDougalls held their islands officially from the King of Norway. King Alexander II (1214–49) came twice to Argyll to give charters of land to local chiefs in an attempt to secure their allegiance. In 1249 he went to Kerrera specifically to try to

Aros Castle, Mull

Gylen Castle, Kerrera

Breachachadh Castle, Coll

persuade Ewan of Argyll to forgo this allegiance. Ewan came to meet him, coming by boat from his castle of Dunollie, but refused the King's request. Alexander was then suddenly stricken, apparently by a fever, and collapsed and died, it is said, as he was mounting his horse.

Alexander III, who succeeded his father, antagonised King Haakon of Norway by sanctioning a brutal raid on the Norwegian-held Isle of Skye. Consequently, in 1263, the Norwegian king equipped the greatest expedition of galleys and men at arms ever known to have left his country. In August that year he anchored with a large part of his fleet of 200 ships in the Firth of Lorn off Kerrera. Ewan of Lorn, although obedient to his summons, refused to join forces with him on the grounds that he held his mainland territory from Alexander III. Haakon, apparently much saddened, raised anchor and put to sea. He rounded the Mull of Kintyre and plundered Bute, Cowal and the Cumbraes. On 2 October King Haakon, with a strong force, landed on the shore at Largs on the Ayrshire coast. There he was attacked by a Scottish army, which drove the invaders back to their ships. The Equinoctial gales were blowing. Many galleys dragged their anchors

and were stranded and the Norwegians were very short of supplies. Haakon decided to return to Norway but died in Orkney on the journey home.

Subsequently, in 1296, the Treaty of Perth, agreed between Alexander III and the King of Norway, allowed all of the Hebridean islands to be leased to Scotland for a down payment of 100 marks[22]. The Chiefs of the Isles, confirmed in possession of their domains, were subjected to the law and custom of Scotland, legislation which proved hard to enforce. The descendants of Somerled, described as 'the barons of Argyll and the Isles', were amongst those confirmed in possession of their land. Most significantly Alexander MacDougall, Lord of Lorn, was entrusted with 'the care and custody of Kintyre, Argyll and Lorn, with responsibility for the King's revenues there.'[23]

The death of Alexander III, whose reign has been described as 'a golden age' is surrounded by superstition. A witch, who he refused to pardon, cursed him and his progeny as she was about to be hanged. Then at Queensferry, when he insisted on crossing the River Forth on a wild night of storm, the ferryman, with second sight, begged him to turn back. All that is known for certain is that once on the Fife coast, his horse either stumbled, throwing him from the cliffs, or else foundered in quicksand on the beach at Kinghorn where he was found dead.

## Fraoch Eilean Castle, Loch Awe

Fraoch Eilean in Gaelic means the Heather Isle. It is one of a group of islands in the north-east end of Loch Awe, towards the mouth of the Pass of Brander, a key position for defence of this very important waterway in Lorn. The castle is first recorded in a charter of 1262 of Alexander III to Gillechrist MacNachden, a member of a prominent local family who held baronial rights. By the terms of the charter, translated from Latin, the MacNaughtons were granted 'custody of our castle and island of Frechelan, so that they should cause the said castle to be built at our expense and repaired as often as necessary, and should keep it safely for our use.' This included the provision of a clean bed of straw when required!

The architecture of the castle, a hall house built of two main storeys with a garret, standing within a curtain wall, is typical of late-13th century date, a feature being the bottle-neck prison in one wall. A later dwelling house, within the original building, was added in the early 17th century. By this time the MacNaughtons had become vassals of the Campbells of Inverawe whose descendants own the island today.

Fraoch Eilean is the scene of a legend of Ossian derived from the Greek myth of the Hesperides. Fraoch, a Finian warrior, fell in love with a beautiful girl on the nearby island of Inistrynich. But her mother, Maeve, furiously jealous, feigned illness and said she must have the fruit of a tree on Fraoch Eilean which had magical healing powers. Fraoch landed and found a serpent coiled round the trunk of the tree. It woke up as he tried to pick the fruit and together they wrestled until, hopelessly entangled, they both drowned in Loch Awe.

### The Rise of Clan Campbell

Following the death of Alexander III in 1286, families in Argyll, as elsewhere in Scotland, became divided in their allegiance to the claimants of the throne. In 1291–92 Alexander MacDougall, Lord of Lorn, or Alexander of Argyll as he was usually called in Scottish records, was one of the forty Scottish auditors nominated by John Balliol of Galloway, one of the two chief Competitors for the Crown – the other being Robert Bruce of Annandale, grandfather of King Robert the Bruce. Significantly Sir Colin Campbell of Loch Awe, known in Scottish records as Cailean Mor, was an auditor for Robert Bruce.

Edward I, when asked to adjudicate, decided in favour of Balliol who ruled from 1292 until 1296. Upon becoming king, Balliol then made Alexander of Argyll, to whom he was related by marriage, his lieutenant or viceroy of the whole of the Western Highlands. The authority exercised by Alexander of Argyll was greatly resented by the Campbells, a clan of rising importance on the middle reaches of Loch Awe.

## Innis Chonnel Castle, Loch Awe

The castle of Innis Chonnell, ruined but still magnificent, stands on an island near the south shore of Loch Awe. This is the first key castle of the Campbells, who are believed to have settled on the shores of Loch Awe through marriage to an heiress of the old Celtic family of O'Duibne. But theories differ as to whether it was

Innis Chonnel Castle, Loch Awe

built by an early member of the family, or acquired by a royal grant from Robert the Bruce.

A stairway from the landing on the south side leads to a vaulted gatehouse, and the entrance to the castle itself is reached by a ramp of earth which probably replaced an earlier drawbridge. A stair leads from the doorway down into a courtyard. The south-east tower dates from the 13th century, arrow slits in the masonry being sited for all-round protection. The west range and the south-west tower were reconstructed during the 15th century, probably by Sir Duncan, later Lord Campbell, of Loch Awe. They comprise a hall and a kitchen set over the range of vaulted cellars, which contained provisions for the garrison, together with a large square angle tower consisting of private rooms. The kitchen was enlarged in the 17th century when the present fireplace was installed. The hall gives way to a lobby, below which lies the vaulted prison, sealed against light and air.

In 1308–09 Innis Chonnel was held by John Bacach of Lorn for Edward II. But following his defeat it was granted, in 1315, by Robert the Bruce, to Colin, son of Sir Neil Campbell, the king's strongest supporter in Argyll. Amongst Sir Neil's descendants at Innis Chonnel Castle was Colin, known as 'Iongantach' or the wonderful, for his amazing achievements. As a young man it is said he had been sleeping in a barn when men of the Clan Callum, who wanted their foster son to succeed to Loch Awe, set fire to it. Colin, waking up to find himself roasting alive in his armour, broke out and, fighting off the men outside, plunged into the Kilmartin Burn where, in 'The Pool of the Lureach' (Pool of the Armour) he lay sizzling as the MacCallums fled.

In 1361 Colin received a grant from his 'cousin' Christian, of her part of her late husband Alexander MacNaughton's barony, in exchange for a sum of money and some cows. Christian had been previously married to MacDougall of Lorn, by whom she had a son, who now, disapproving his mother's behaviour, kept her a prisoner at Dunollie. One night she managed to escape and by some means or other to reach the north shore of Loch Awe. From there, knowing her son was on her heels, she shouted across to the castle for a boat. It came, but as she was climbing into it her son fired an arrow which pierced her thigh to the side of the boat. Mad with pain and anger she cursed him in Gaelic words meaning: 'You with the white bow that frisk upon yonder shore, pray God I may

hear the noise of the Fowls of the air feeding, or picking on your face.' Her son was duly killed by men of Craignish from whom he was trying to extract some rents. Meanwhile Christian had fallen in love with young MacIver of Asknish, a servitor of Colin Iongantach. She wanted to marry him but Colin, in giving his permission, drove a hard bargain, forcing her to resign her lands of Craignish to himself before he would agree to her request. The deal was arranged in November 1361.

The 1st Earl of Argyll, who died in 1493, made Inveraray his main residence. In 1499 his son, Earl Archibald, and Hugh Rose of Kilravock, were declared guardians of the little Muriel, daughter and heiress of the Thane of Cawdor. At harvest time Earl Archibald sent 60 men, commanded by Campbell of Inverliever, to bring the child to Argyll. Someone apparently pointed out to Inverliever that she was not yet married and could easily fail to survive, whereupon Inverliever famously retorted that 'Muriel can never die while there is a red-haired lassie on the shores of Loch Awe!'

Inverliever galloped away with little Muriel's uncles in hot pursuit. 'S fhada glaodh a Lochow! 'It's a far cry to Loch Awe,' the famous saying sprang from the chase. The uncles, with a larger force, were gaining, but reaching a cornfield, Inverliever had the brilliant idea of wrapping a stook in a shawl to look like a small child. His men stood round it, dying in a desperate defence, which gave him long enough, with the child on the pommel of his saddle, to ride full tilt for the safety of Argyll. Held either in Innis Chonnel or Inveraray, she eventually married Sir John Campbell of Calder, son of the 2nd Earl, their union proving, surprisingly, to be a happy one.

Innis Chonnel was held by Hereditary Captains, who were martys, or overseers of Lower Loch Awe. The castle was then used mainly as a prison. Argyll's grandson, Donald Dubh, was held here for 19 years until rescued by MacDonalds of Glencoe (see p. 41).[24]

A MacArthur captain was dismissed for dishonesty in 1631. MacLachlans then held the appointment. In 1746, Young McLachlan of Innis Chonnel, called out by his chief, Lachlan MacLachlan of MacLachlan to fight for Prince Charles, was galloping down the line at the battle of Culloden, carrying the order for the Highland regiments to charge, when a cannon ball took off his head. The MacLachlans remained Captains of Innis Chonnel until c1815, but the castle was abandoned as a residence early in the 18th century.

## Craignish Castle

The castle of Craignish at the head of Loch Beag, overlooking the Sound of Jura, was sited to defend the Craignish Peninsula from attack from the sea. The walls of the original tower house, built in the late 13th or early 14th century, are incorporated in the present building. The old castle is mentioned as being unfinished in 1414.

The first Campbell of Craignish is believed to have married the heiress of the Celtic Thane of Loch Avich, which lies to the north of Loch Awe. The barony of Craignish was granted to Dugald Campbell by David II. His daughter Christian, a lady of doubtful reputation, carried on a liaison with Colin Iongatach (Colin the Wonderful), Sir Colin Campbell of Lochawe. Reduced eventually to penury, she sold him her inheritance in return for promised support.

In 1646, Alasdair MacColla MacDonald laid siege to the castle. Repulsed, he went off saying 'that is a strong castle of whelks, the wind itself is the only thing that will keep up a constant fight with it!'[25] Some alterations were made to Craignish in the 15th and 16th centuries, but the castle as we see it today is largely the result of the reconstruction, carried out in 1837, by the architect William Burn.

The castle is not open to the public.

## Caisteal na Nighinn Ruaidhe
## The Castle of the Red-haired Girl

Sometime towards the end of the 12th century Brigid, daughter of Dugal MacCaurrie, the *toiseach* (chief) of Lochavich to the north of Loch Awe, married Dougall Campbell of Craignish near to the village of Ardfern. The castle on the island in Loch Avich was probably built by their son, or grandson, in about 1250. The story connected with the building comes from Lord Archibald Campbell's Records of Argyll.

The story goes that there was once a builder in Edinburgh who had an only son. Having agreed to build a castle in Argyll he set off with the boy, to whom his mother said on parting, 'Be sure to have a sweetheart where you are going.' Subsequently, on reaching Loch Avich, the boy fell in love with a red-haired girl who worked in the house where the Campbells were living while their castle was built. Once it was finished, seeing her obviously worried, he asked her what was wrong. She whispered that her master intended to kill him as he could not afford to pay for the work that had been done. She begged him not to reveal what she had told him for she knew that the laird would kill her if he found out what she had done. The young man went to his father, who promised to defeat the evil scheme. Next morning he stood in

Craignish Castle

front of the castle gazing intently at the walls. Along came Campbell, asking him what he was doing, and he told him, 'I am looking at a stone that has been placed askew. It will bring down the whole building unless it is taken out.'

'Then,' thundered Campbell, 'let it be removed.'

'Alas,' said the builder, 'I must have a special hammer which I left behind in Edinburgh.'

The laird said he would send a man to get it, but the builder protested that it was so valuable that his wife would not part with it unless Campbell's own son and heir went to fetch it himself. Campbell reluctantly agreed. His son went off bearing a letter from the builder to his wife reading, 'I have sent to you the little hammer, and do not part with it until the big hammer comes home.'

The wife, understanding, clapped the unfortunate young Campbell in prison where he stayed until both her husband and son were safely back in Edinburgh. Meanwhile, in his newly built castle on Loch Avich, Campbell realised what had happened. Insane with rage he dragged the unfortunate red-haired girl to the parapet and threw her to her death on the rocks below. But from this time on there was no peace in the castle. On dark and stormy nights, torches were seen on the battlements and a long ghastly scream rang out from above the walls.

Fincharn Castle

On the other side of Loch Awe, almost opposite Loch Avich, another fortress greatly similar to Caisteal na Nighinn Ruaidhe was one of the three castles built by the MacDougalls to defend the great inland waterway of their Lordship. Held by the Campbells following their conquest of Loch Awe, the castle passed through marriage to the Scrymgeours, whose ancestor Alexander, Constable of Dundee, was Bruce's standard bearer at the Battle of Bannockburn in 1314. A later laird, John Scrymgeour, is said to have used his 'droit de seigneur' to ravish the bride of one of his tenants. Her family waited for their revenge until, as a wedding which he attended was taking place, they set fire to the castle of which only a shell remains.

## CARN CAILEAN, THE MURDER OF CAILEAN MOR

According to local tradition, a dispute arose about the march between the Campbells' lands and those of the MacDougalls on the north shore of the loch. A meeting was arranged by a burn called Allt a' Chomhlachaidh (Stream of the Conference), which crosses the old road, the Sreang Lathurnach (the String of Lorn) near the head of Glen Scammadale.

Accounts differ as to what took place. Some say that the MacDougalls, distracted by a seer who predicted a disastrous result, failed to arrive in time, and the Campbells continued down the glen and encountered them at the Allt an Ath'Dhearg (Stream of the Red Ford), where a fierce and bloody conflict took place. But, according to *Ane Accompt*, Sir Colin had put the MacDougalls to flight and was chasing them across the ford when he was killed.[26] The Campbells appeared to be gaining, but a MacDougall crept up behind a rock, called the Carn of Cailean (the Cairn of Colin) and shot the fatal arrow which killed the Campbell chief.

Cailean Mor, who lies buried in Kilchrenan, was the ancestor of the Duke of Argyll.

## THE WAR OF INDEPENDENCE

Alexander III died in 1285 leaving only his granddaughter, the little 'Maid of Norway', as his heir. Scotland, Norway and England all favoured a marriage between this little girl (daughter of Alexander's daughter who married King Eric of Norway) and Edward I of England's son the first Prince of Wales. The arrangement was concluded by the Treaty of Birnham-on-Tweed in July 1290, when Edward cunningly contrived a clause to the effect that, in the event of either his son or Margaret dying childless, he himself would inherit the kingship of Scotland which would then descend to his heirs. His ambition was soon realised when, only two months later, the 'Maid of Norway' died in Orkney on her journey home to Scotland.

John Balliol, grandson of David Earl of Huntingdon (brother of King Malcolm IV) and Robert Bruce of Carrick, a great-grandson, were foremost amongst the many claimants to the Scottish throne. Edward of England, asked to adjudicate, summoned the Scottish lords to Norham, in Northumberland, where significantly Alexander of Lorn, Lord of Argyll, stood security for Balliol, to whom he was related, while Sir Colin Campbell, Cailean Mor, acted in the same capacity for Bruce.

Balliol, accepting King Edward's suzerainty, ruled as his vassal until he renounced his homage to him, in April 1296. Edward had by then invaded Scotland and Balliol surrendered to him in July. Edward marched as far north as Elgin and returned to England with many Scottish treasures including 'The Stone of Destiny', which he took from Scone. Before leaving he arranged a government for Scotland, similar to that already established in Wales. The Scots detested the tyranny to which they were subjected. William Wallace, son of a Renfrewshire knight, headed a rebellion. He won a glorious victory at the battle of Stirling Bridge, in 1297, but was ultimately defeated at the battle of Falkirk in the same year. In 1305 he was taken prisoner and brutally executed in London.

Following the abdication of John Balliol in 1296, Alexander of Argyll adhered initially to Robert the Bruce. In 1301 Alexander's son John Bacach (Lame John) is reported as laying siege to Castle Suibhne, key fortress of Knapdale, which was held by Alexander MacDonald, of Islay and Kintyre, for Edward I. It was only when Bruce murdered Alexander's nephew, the 'Red Comyn', in Greyfriars Church in Dumfries in 1306, that Alexander of Lorn, in understandable fury, declared for the English King.

In June 1306 Robert the Bruce was defeated by an English army, commanded by Aymer de Valence, at Methven, west of Perth. He retreated into Strathfillan where, on 11 August, near Tyndrum, he was confronted by a large force of MacDougalls said to have numbered 1,000 men, commanded by Alexander's son John Bacach (the lame). The site of the battle is known as Dal Righ, meaning 'Field of the King'.

Bruce, fighting with the rearguard of his army, found himself trapped on a path beside Lochan nan Arm (Loch of the Arms) too narrow for his horse to turn. Seeing him trapped, three of MacDougall's men, two of them brothers named Mac na Dorsair, leapt on him from the bank above. Bruce rose to his full height in the stirrups. Light flashed from the great crystal brooch on his shoulder and from the blade of his sword. With a blow he severed the arm of the man gripping the bridle but instantly another grabbed his leg to unhorse him. Spurring the animal forward he dragged him, his hand trapped by the stirrup to

the flank. A third man jumped from the bank on to the horse's rump, clasping the king's cloak to his sides. Struggling to free his sword, Bruce struck backwards with the pommel, sending him flying with a force that split his skull as it hit the ground. Then, as his arm came free, he swung round in his saddle to fell the man, held by the stirrup, at his side. Simultaneously, as the man behind him fell, he pulled the cloak from his shoulders. With it came the brooch, holding the great crystal, which has remained an heirloom of the chiefs of the Clan MacDougall to the present day.

Guided by Sir Neil Campbell, his strongest supporter in Argyll, Bruce reached Loch Lomond, from where he made his way to the Clyde. Sir Neil Campbell, in one of his small fleet of galleys, ferried him across to Arran from where, in a small boat, he crossed Kilbrannan Sound. Landing at Ugadale, on the east coast of Kintyre, he met Ferquhard MacKay, who, despite his ragged clothing, knew him by his height and bearing to be an important man. MacKay guided him across the peninsula and once in sight of the sea pointed out the way he should go. As they said farewell the King took the brooch from his mantle and, giving it to him, asked what he wanted as a reward. 'To own the land that I now farm as a tenant,' came the reply. Then, he killed a sheep and skinned it, to draw the two farms on the hide. Later, Bruce kept his word. The original grant on the sheepskin, about three inches square, bears the words: 'I, Robert the First, give the lands of Ugadale and Arnicle to MacKay and his heirs forever.' The formal charter, dated 31 March 1329, was renewed in the reign of James IV.

The Ugadale brooch, which greatly resembles the Brooch of Lorn, has an outer band decorated with strap work. Within it eight turrets, set with coral and pearls, alternate with small round bosses. The oval ridged crystal in the middle is set on the lid of a capsule ornamented with filigree. It opens to reveal a relic container almost exactly similar to that of the Brooch of Lorn.

From Kintyre, at Dunaverty, Bruce reached Rathlin Island. From there he returned to Scotland to begin the campaign which made him virtually the master of Scotland by the spring of 1308. Only in Argyll did Alexander of Argyll continue to defy him. Alexander's son, John Bacach, wrote to Edward II in April or May appealing for help. He told him he stood alone, 'For the barons of Argyll give me no aid,'

The Pass of Brander

and that with only 500 men he was struggling to hold three castles and a lake 24 miles long, which is taken to be Loch Awe and the castles of Fraoch Eilean, Innis Chonnel and Fincharn. But no assistance came and in August, John Bacach struggled from his bed of sickness at Dunstaffnage, to organise defence against the advancing army.

Bruce reached Loch Awe, it would seem without opposition. But the eastern end of the loch was held by the MacNaughtons – allies of the MacDougalls – from their castle on the island of Fraoch Eilean.

### The Battle of the pass of Brander

The Pass of Brander is a fissure in the rocks, resulting from the great thaw that occurred at the end of the last Ice Age. Now, faced as he was by hostile forces, Bruce saw a way to turn this natural bottleneck to his own advantage. He accordingly divided his force, sending some men by boat across Loch Awe. Landing on the north shore they followed Glen Nant to reinforce Sir Neil Campbell, Bruce's strongest supporter in Argyll, who was converging upon the western exit of the pass. At the same time the King commanded Sir James, the Black Douglas, to lead a party of Highlanders, clad only in deerskins in place of heavy armour, up the shoulder of Cruachan to a point above the enemy.

The battle began as Bruce, with the greater part of his army, advanced into the pass from the east. Then as his men scrambled forward along the narrow and precipitous path, with deep water below them, the forces of John Bacach, hidden amongst the scrub on the hillside, made their attack. But as they moved, the Highlanders, led by Douglas, hurling rocks and boulders before them, charged down from above. The MacDougalls were totally defeated and cairns on the south side of the River Awe (below the Hydro Electric Barrage) reputedly cover their graves.

### The Council of Ardchattan

Bruce then laid siege to Dunstaffnage, where Alexander of Argyll, on surrender, was allowed to make honourable submission. He is believed to have been one of the local chiefs who were summoned by King Robert the Bruce to attend a Council at Ardchattan Priory, on the north shore of Loch Etive, in 1309. The transactions conducted in Gaelic were translated for the King to understand.

### Forefeiture of MacDougalls of Lorn

Alexander is known to have attended the St Andrews Parliament, convened by the king in March 1309, but he seems to have left Scotland shortly afterwards and died, either in England or in Ireland, in 1310. John Bacach fled to England to become a vassal of Edward

II. He was not in medieval law a traitor, having never sworn loyalty to Bruce, the murderer of his nephew, the Red Comyn. John died in 1317.

Following his defeat of Alexander of Argyll King Robert the Bruce granted his island possessions, including Mull, Coll and Tiree, as well as the mainland districts of Morvern, Ardgour and Glencoe, to Angus MacDonald of Kintyre and the Isles. The Lordship of Lorn was restored to John Bacach's son Ewan, between 1330 and 1335, but the island possessions, with the exception of Kerrera, were never returned.

*Increasing Ascendency of Clan Campbell*

Sir Neil Campbell of Lochawe, Bruce's strongest supporter in mainland Argyll, also received territorial reward. During the 14th century the chiefs of Clan Campbell became overlords of much of the district of Cowal. In 1334 Sir Colin Campbell, son of Sir Neil, defeated the English at Dunoon, and was made Hereditary Governor of the Castle, an honour which has descended to the present Duke of Argyll.

In 1424 Sir Duncan Campbell of Loch Awe was the richest in land of the hostages held in England as security for the ransom of James I of Scotland. King James on his return made him Lieutenant of Argyll and a Privy Councillor. Later he became Justice General and, in the reign of James II, a Lord of Parliament.

In the mid-15th century Duncan, Lord Campbell, acquired the superiority of both Glenstrae and Glenorchy, hereditary territory of Clan Gregor. He gave Glenorchy to Colin, son of his second marriage, whose descendants became Earls of Breadalbane. Lord Campbell's eldest son by his first marriage pre-deceased him but his grandson Colin, who succeeded him as the 2nd Lord Campbell, was created Earl of Argyll by James II of Scotland in 1457.

## CASTLES OF THE CAMPBELLS OF GLENORCHY

### Kilchurn Castle, Lochawe

*Child of loud-throated War! the mountain stream*
*Roars in thy hearing; but thy hour of rest*
*Is come, and thou art silent in thy age*
*Save when the wind sweeps by and sounds are caught.*

So wrote William Wordsworth in 1803 when, from above Dalmally, he first caught sight of Kilchurn. The castle, at the east end of Loch Awe, was built by Sir Colin Campbell 1st of Glenorchy (son by his second marriage of Duncan Lord Campbell) *c*1440. Sir Colin was a Knight of Rhodes and traditionally the original tower house and courtyard were completed by his wife while he was fighting the Infidel, alongside

Kilchurn Castle

the Knights of Rhodes, in Spain.

A story is told that on the eve of his departure he cut his wife's wedding ring in half. Keeping part of it himself, he told her that she must consider herself a widow should he not return within seven years. The allotted time passed with no sign of him, and urged by her father, she agreed to marry the Baron of Phantisland, near Kilchrenan, on the nearby north shore of Loch Awe. On the night before the wedding the castle blazed with lights. A tramp asked an old woman in a cottage at Succoth, south-east of Dalmally, for the reason. She told him and he went to the castle to claim a drink of wine from the bride as was customary at that time. She came to the door and handed him a goblet. He quaffed down the wine and handed back the empty goblet. In the bottom was his half of the ring. This intriguing tale may carry a spark of truth. Quarreling between the Campbells of Glenorchy and the MacCorquodales of Phantisland is documented at that time.

The first Colin's descendent, 'Grey Colin', 6th of Glenorchy, rebuilt the top of the tower house and added the corbelled angle rounds. Sir Colin was succeeded by his son, 'Black Duncan of the Cowl', 7th of Glenorchy, who reconstructed the south-west range, containing the laich hall and the kitchen, between 1614–16.

In 1654 Sir John Campbell of Glenorchy and the Marquess of Argyll, besieged in Kilchurn by the Royalist General Middleton, were rescued by General Monck. Sir John's son, of the same name, married the heiress of the Earl of Holland and was created Earl of Breadalbane and Holland by Charles II in 1681. Following her death he married Mary, daughter of the Marquess of Argyll, and widow of the Earl of Caithness. The initials E.I.B. and C.M.C. on the armorial shield above the entrance stand for Johanes (John) Earl of Breadalbane and Mary, Countess of Caithness.

In 1690, Breadalbane, at the bequest of William III, added the two ranges of four-storeyed barracks on the north side of the castle. Kilchurn, although repaired and garrisoned during the Jacobite Rising of 1745, later became ruinous. Taken over by the then Department of the Environment in 1953, it has since been greatly restored. During the mid 1980s it was sold by the late Countess of Breadalbane. It now belongs to local businessman Mr Ian Cleaver, who plans to maintain the castle as it stands.

## Achallader Castle

This castle, which stands about a mile east of Loch Tulla, at the head of Glen Orchy, was originally built by the Fletchers of Glenorchy. They lost their land to the Campbells of Glenorchy. The now largely ruined tower was constructed by Sir Duncan Campbell, 7th of Glenorchy (Black Duncan of the Cowl) in the late 16th century. Burned by resentful MacGregors in 1603[27], the castle was then rebuilt.

In the autumn of 1621, John Earl of Mar, Lord High Treasurer of Scotland, was invited by 'Black Duncan of the Cowl' to take part in a deer hunt in the forest of Coireach a'Bà on the Black Mount. Deer hunts in the 17th century were important events. Ghillies spread a cordon round a large area. They then drove all animals before them, including wild cats and wolves, into wooden palisades, or in the high mountains natural enclosures. On this particular occasion they were herded into Coire an Easain (hollow of the waterfalls), which lies to the south of Meall a Bhùiridh. (The White Corries ski lift is on the northeast side.) Men with hagbuts, bows and arrows and hounds waited hidden below the entrance to the Coire through which the beasts would come. Once trapped the deer were slaughtered to fill the brine tubs with venison, which saved Highland families from starvation throughout the winter months. The number of deer killed that autumn of 1621 is now long since forgotten. All that is remembered is the snow-white hind that got away.

Mar reported this phenomenon to King James VI who, greatly excited, decided that whatever the difficulties, he must have the white deer in Windsor Park. Delighted at the project, he summoned a man called John Scandaver, a forester practised in netting deer (this being the easiest way to catch them) who with two assistants set out in the depth of winter to capture the white hind of Coireach a'Bà.

Arriving in Edinburgh they were joined by Sir Duncan Campbell's second son, Robert Campbell of Glenfalloch, who, at Mar's request, agreed to be their guide. With him they traveled west until they reached Achallader, then used as a hunting lodge. Here they were well entertained, Sir Duncan assuring Mar that they had the best that could be found in the country at that time of year, 'and want neither wine or acquavitae.' Happily would they have stayed in the castle, but this was not the reason for their quest.

The white hind had been seen again in Coire an Easain. Therefore, on the morning of 22 February, ignoring the insistence of the local forester that she could never be taken without at least two thousand men, the would-be captors set off. The weather was terrible, 'so vehement and the way so evill and rogh,' as Sir Duncan reported. After an exhausting climb they at last reached the entrance to Coire an Easain. This was the haunt of their quarry but Scandaver, an old man, declaring he could 'go no further, aither on fute or horse,' was utterly spent.

His two assistants, however, together with Robert Campbell, continued to clamber up the mountain for a distance of about another mile. The mist thickened. Then for a moment a shaft of sunlight broke through the clouds. There above them stood a herd of deer, amongst them a hind 'als quheit as ane quheit scheip'. The deer hunters returned defeated, terrified of the King's rage. But Sir Duncan sent him a present of a capercailzie, with which he was so delighted that he quite forgot the white hind!

The castle was again sacked by Jacobite soldiers, returning from the battle of Killiecrankie, in 1689. This time the damage was so great that two years later, John Earl of Breadalbane, Sir Duncan's descendant, set up a tented camp to house a conference held there in 1691. The 'Treaty of Achallader' was signed on 30 June 1691 by Major General Buchan and Sir George Barclay on behalf of the Jacobites, and by Breadalbane for the Government (see p. 76).

## Barcaldine Castle

The six merklands of Barcaldine were included in the third part of Lorn which was granted by Colin, 1st Earl of Argyll, to his uncle, Sir Colin Campbell, 1st of Glenorchy, in 1470.[28] Barcaldine, known as 'The Black Castle' was built by Sir Duncan Campbell, 7th of Glenorchy, for five thousand marks in 1601[29] as an outpost of the north-west portion of his vast estate. It stands in a strategic position, between Loch Etive and Loch Creran, about a mile north-west of the village of Benderloch, and some four miles from Connel Bridge, which spans the narrows called the Falls of Lora, crossed by a ferry in Sir Duncan's day. The L-plan tower house contains three storeys and an attic. The four turrets at the corners of the tower hold pistol holes, as do the main walls.

In 1699, John 1st Earl of Breadalbane granted

Achallader Castle

the castle in feu to Alexander Campbell. Repairs were carried out but the Campbells of Barcaldine moved to Barcaldine House, which they built in 1724. Barcaldine Castle then became a ruin. The estate was sold but bought back by Sir Duncan Campbell, 3rd Baronet of Barcaldine, who restored the castle in 1911. His sister is said to haunt it. She can be heard playing the piano on windy nights.

Sold by the Campbells of Barcaldine in 2009 to Mr David Whitehead, the castle is now a bed-and-breakfast establishment.

## THE AQUISITION OF THE LORDSHIP OF LORN BY COLIN, 1ST EARL OF ARGYLL

### The Stewarts of Appin

Duncan, Lord Campbell of Loch Awe, died in 1453. His grandson Colin, who succeeded him, was created Earl of Argyll by James II in 1457. The dramatic story of how the Lordship of Lorn passed into his possession has already been told. Dugald Stewart, whose claim to the lordship was refuted by the Privy Council, eventually received Appin directly from the Crown. Mr Andrew Stewart, his descendant, is 17th chief of the Stewarts of Appin today.

### Castle Stalker

Castle Stalker, or more correctly Castle Stalcair, the castle of the Hunter, on its tiny island in Loch Laich, is a famous landmark of Appin. The castle is believed to have been built by Alan Stewart of Appin in the mid-16th century, although, according to another source, it was granted to him by James V, who died in 1542. The lands of Appin, lying west and south of the village, were sold by Duncan Stewart of Appin to Sir Donald Campbell of Ardnamurchan and Airds in 1620.

According to a well-known tradition the Stewarts then lost Castle Stalker when the young chief Duncan, 7th of Appin, known as Duncan 'Baothaire' (Weak-minded) exchanged it during a drinking bout for a birlinn (an eight-oared galley) with Donald Campbell of Ardnamurchan and Airds. The New Statistical Account of 1845 states that the building was 'new roofed and floored' by Sir Donald Campbell of Ardnamurchan in 1631.

In 1686, following the execution of the 9th Earl of Argyll, the Stewarts regained the castle for a brief four years. But forfeited as Jacobites in 1690, they were forced to surrender it to the Crown. In 1745, when word of Prince Charles Edward's landing in Moidart reached Inveraray, Castle Stalker was garrisoned by the 3rd Duke of Argyll. The castle, by then roofless, was sold by the Campbells in the mid-19th century. Re-purchased by Stewarts in 1908 it was then bought by Colonel Stewart Allward in 1966, who restored it much to its original form.

The castle is open by private arrangement only.

## SUMMARY OF MAIN EVENTS 1329–1411 THE LORDSHIP OF THE ISLES

During the 14th and early 15th centuries the MacDonalds of the Isles, largely through fortuitous marriages, had achieved not only the superiority of the Western Isles as far north as Lewis, but also territories on the mainland from Kintyre to the borders of Caithness.

Angus of the Isles, who died in 1329, was succeeded by his eldest son John, known as 'Good John of Islay', described by contemporaries as the most magnificent man alive. John married twice. His first wife was Amie MacRuairi, heiress to the islands of Uist, Barra, Rum and Eigg, as well as part of Garmoran on the mainland. This union ended in divorce and John then married Margaret, daughter of Robert the Steward, who became Robert II.

The settlement between them included the agreement that by renouncing his claim to the 'Kingship of the Isles', a title descending through Somerled, he should adopt that of 'Dominus de Insulis', otherwise Lord of the Isles. Likewise it was stipulated that while Amie's lands should descend to her sons (Ranald, the ancestor of the MacDonalds of Clanranald and Glengarry and Godfrey, patronymic founder of his clan), those of the Lordship should be inherited by the sons of Princess Margaret. Consequently Donald the eldest came into the greater part, but Kintyre and the south of Islay went to his brother, known as John Mor Tanister (Tanister meaning 'elected heir to a position').

Both brothers then married heiresses. Donald's wife Mary was, in her own right, the Countess of Ross, the enormous territory in the north of Scotland, which thus became part of the Lordship. By marrying Marjory Bissett, of the Seven Glens of Antrim, John achieved an acquisition of land which proved of polit-

*Finlaggan*

Moonlight piercing through the mist
catches the castle tower.
The Lord of the Isles is he feasting there
as happened long ago?
And is the sentry watchful still
in this the danger hour?
While men at arms sleep fitfully
within the hall below.

A dog barks high upon the hill
a wolf or chasing hound?
And does a man gasp terrified
to know he is pursued?
Stumbling and crying does he fall on
      rock-strewn alien ground?
Knowing his life must surely pay for
      long and bloodstained feud.

Then with the light comes gentle wind,
the ruin stands alone.
A curlew calls, a single swan
flies into rising day.
There is no voice, no sign of men
to meet the coming dawn.
The ruins on the island stand,
they do not fade away

ical significance in the history of Northern Ireland. The family, thereafter, were styled 'of Dunyvaig and the Glens'.

*Finlaggan*
*Seat of the Lords of the Isles*

Loch Finlaggan lies in the north-east of Islay, some 4.5km from Port Askaig. Today, if you go there in winter, geese rise at your approach, and in summer swans nest undisturbed amongst tall rustling reeds. Now it is hard to believe that this was once the nucleus of a dynasty, which rivalled that of the kings.

Two islands lie in the northern end of the loch. The largest, Eilean Mor is divided from the shore by a narrow channel. Here stand the ruins of the castle of the MacDonald Lord of the Isles, thought to have

been built during the time of Angus II, who died *c*1330. The remains of the family chapel and foundations of other buildings which remain on the island are apparently of the same date. Close to the chapel an ancient cemetery is believed to contain the graves of the wives and children of the Lords of the Isles, who themselves were buried in Iona. The smaller island of Eilean na Comhairle, once connected to Eilean Mor by a causeway, was the seat of the Council Chamber where the business of the Lordship was discussed.

Another island at the southern end of the loch was probably a prison. Traditionally the blood hounds were housed on the nearby shore so that anyone attempting to escape could be quickly run down. Traces of the barracks of the private army, the 'fiery tail' of the Lord of the Isles, lie on the same eastern shore and these, together with the other ruins, prove the enormous amount of activity that once existed here.

The family residence probably stood at the southern end of Eilean Mor. Now only traces remain of what must have been a substantial and probably impressive house. But within the great hall 'Good John of Islay', so renowned for his munificence, must have dined with his family and retainers while the bards recited the lineage of the MacDonalds and minstrels played to entertain. Also it was here that John's son Donald discovered 'The Mammet of Islay', who he claimed to be Richard II.

The reason for this deception resulted from a quarrel between Donald and the Duke of Albany (Regent from 1406–20, during the imprisonment of James I) over possession of the Earldom of Ross. Donald had married Mary Leslie, younger daughter and supposed heiress of the Earl of Ross, but Albany claimed that her elder sister Euphemia had bequeathed it to him before retiring to a monastery. Donald tried to blackmail the English King, Henry IV, into supporting him by exploiting the then current rumours of the whereabouts of Richard II. Richard, having been deposed by Henry, was almost certainly murdered in Pontefract Castle, but Donald, finding a red-haired scullion who resembled him in his kitchen at Finlaggan, proclaimed that he was giving him sanctuary. The 'Mammet of Islay' was certainly an impostor, for no one who knew Richard ever appears to have seen him. Consequently the hoped-for aid from England never materialised.

Following the resignation by John II, Lord of

Finlaggan

the growing rivalry between the Campbells and the MacDonalds for mastery in the West Highlands. Therefore it seems to have been no accident that the envoy he sent to deal with John Mor Tanister on Islay was one James Campbell. They met at a rendezvous, attended by armed escorts. Inevitably a quarrel began. Swords flew from their scabbards, and in the ensuing scrimmage, John Mor Tanister was killed. Campbell, on returning to the mainland, was tried and executed at Inverness, the king denying all involvement. The treacherous killing of John Mor Tanister created intense animosity between the MacDonalds of the Isles and the ruling house of Stewart. In 1431 John's son Donald Balloch, appointed at the age of eighteen to take his place, defeated the Royal Army at Inverlochy and laid waste to the area.

King James I reputedly then led an army into Argyll but, upon reaching Dunstaffnage, found that Balloch had retreated to Islay. The king, without a fleet of his own, left the punishment of the islanders to local people and he later received a head, supposed to be that of Balloch, in proof of his reported death. King James himself was murdered in 1437. In the consequent connivance amongst families struggling for power, Alexander, Lord of the Isles and Earl of Ross, signed an agreement of mutual support with the Earls of Douglas and Crawford c1445. This, in his case, proved a formality, but the consequent involvement of his son, John II, Lord of the Isles, with the 9th Earl of Douglas, was to have fatal consequences for his family.

James, 9th Earl of Douglas, defeated by King James II in 1455, fled to England to swear loyalty to the Duke of York, who became Edward IV. The theory that he returned to Scotland to confer with John, Lord of the Isles and Donald Balloch is unproven, but Balloch seized the opportunity to make reprisals against the enemies of the Douglasses. In July he sailed from Islay with 100 galleys and a force of 5,000 men. Firstly he laid waste to the lands of Bishop Turnbull of Glasgow, who had lent money to the king to finance his defeat of the Douglasses. Then he returned to Islay, to land his spoil at Port Askaig, before setting course north-eastwards for the green island of Lismore.

This time his quarry was the Bishop of Argyll, George Lauder, who had set his seal to the document ordering the forfeiture of the Douglasses. He himself, warned of the fleet approaching, found sanctuary within his cathedral, but torches were put to the

the Isles, of all his rights to King James IV in 1493, the island settlement in Loch Finlaggan appears to have been abandoned and many of the buildings were, quite probably, destroyed. In the early 1990s, a most interesting museum was built beside the loch by the Friends of Finlaggan, a group of local enthusiasts, who have now built a bridge by which people can cross to Eilean Mor.

## SUMMARY OF MAIN EVENTS 1411–1460

In 1411, the quarrel between Donald Lord of the Isles and the Regent Albany culminated in the Battle of Harlaw in Aberdeenshire. The outcome was indecisive, but Donald eventually surrendered his sword to Albany at Lochgilp (now Lochgilphead) in 1412. Donald's son Alexander, however, was acknowledged as the Earl of Ross by James I, and it was the surrender of that territory by John II, Lord of the Isles (son of Alexander) in 1457 which ignited the disastrous quarrel that brought ruination to the family.

Donald, Lord of the Isles, died in 1423, just before King James I was released from imprisonment in England. Donald's son Alexander succeeded as a minor, and John Mor Tanister was appointed by the Council of the Isles to administer the Lordship until he attained his majority.

King James, a shrewd manipulator, was aware of

thatch of the farmsteads, the animals were slaughtered and stolen and the crops, upon which life depended, were ruthlessly destroyed.[30]

James II attempted reprisals. The cost of shipping cannons, presumably to Islay, is shown in the Exchequer Rolls.[31] But nothing proves that they were landed or that they were actually used. John II, Lord of the Isles, was pardoned by King James II and thereafter remained obedient throughout the rest of his reign.

In 1460 when the king led an army against the English, John with a force of his own men is said to have commanded the right flank, hereditary place of honour of the Lord of the Isles since Bruce's victory at Bannockburn in 1314. Tragically the king was killed at Roxburgh by one of his own cannons exploding as he was inspecting his ordnance before laying siege to the fortress.

## THE TREATY OF ARDTORNISH

Following the death of James II the Douglas ambitions were revived. James, 9th Earl of Douglas, as an exile in England, had sworn fealty to Edward IV. Now, on his instigation, a writ had been issued at Westminster to empower him and his surviving brother, Douglas of Balveny, together with three others, to treat with the Lord of the Isles and Donald Balloch. On 19 October 1461 the vassals of the Lord of the Isles were summoned to a convention in the Castle of Ardtornish, in Morvern on the Sound of Mull. The main items of business concerned the formula of the proposals to be submitted to the English delegates, and the appointment of two commissioners who would travel to London to deal with the matter involved.

The choice devolved upon two men, Ranald Ban, a younger brother of Donald Balloch and Duncan, Archdean of the Isles. They journeyed, almost certainly by sea, to Westminster, where those appointed to treat with them included Lawrence, Bishop of Durham, and Robert Stillington, keeper of the King's Seal. The Treaty of Ardtornish, or the Treaty of London as it is more frequently called, dated at Westminster on 13 February 1462, was one of the worst acts of treachery ever committed against the Scottish State. By its terms the country, once conquered, was to be divided north of the Forth between John, Lord of the Isles and Earl of Ross, Donald Balloch, John, the latter's son and heir, and the Earl of Douglas as vassals of the English King.

Douglas would also regain his estates in the southern parts of Scotland. In addition to this, from Whitsuntide 1462, the Lord of the Isles was to receive from King Edward a hundred marks yearly in time of peace and £200 in time of war. Donald Balloch would receive £20 in peacetime and £40 in wartime and his son half of those amounts. Twelve years later, in the course of diplomatic relations, the fatal document was revealed. John Lord of the Isles and Earl of Ross was condemned for treachery by King James III. He only achieved a pardon by resigning both the earldom of Ross and the whole of Kintyre to the Crown.

### The end of the Lordship of the Isles

John II, Lord of the Isles, had no legitimate children, but his natural son Angus was regarded by the Islesmen as his heir. Angus, bitterly resentful of his father's resignation of the earldom, achieved a strong following amongst some of the chiefs of the Isles. A struggle for supremacy developed, which, in 1482, resulted in the great sea battle of Bloody Bay, off the north-east coast of Mull.

Angus emerged victorious, but on sailing home to Islay, he discovered that his wife and baby son, known as Donald Dubh, had been kidnapped from Finlaggan. He soon knew his father-in-law, Colin, 1st Earl of Argyll to be responsible, discovering that he had sent men of Atholl to Islay to abduct them in the absence of the fighting men. Angus himself was murdered, and Donald Dubh, considered throughout the islands as the rightful heir to the Lordship, remained a prisoner in his maternal grandfather's castle of Innis Chonnel, on an island in Loch Awe, throughout the years of his youth.[32]

John, Lord of the Isles, on the death of his natural son Angus, c1489, gave control of the Lordship to his nephew Alexander of Lochalsh. But in 1491, while making a raid of reprisal into the Earldom of Ross, Alexander was defeated with great loss by the MacKenzies. This proved the final heartbreak for John II, Lord of the Isles, who ended his life in a monastery. In 1493 the lands and titles of the Lordship were forfeited to King James IV.

Thus ended the dynasty, founded by Somerled over 300 years before. John was the last MacDonald to be recognised officially as the Lord of the Isles, a title which, descending through James IV, has now devolved upon Prince Charles.

# CHAPTER 3: Sacred Stones

## THE PRE-REFORMATION CHURCHES AND THE SCULPTURED MONUMENTS OF ARGYLL AND THE ISLES

The carvings on crosses and grave slabs, of Pre-Reformation date, are amongst the greatest treasures of the heritage of Argyll. Some of the beautiful Celtic designs are thought to have been introduced by the Iron Age settlers who are believed to have come from central Europe. Others would seem to have been copied from monuments in the churches seen by the Irish monks, who travelled extensively to the countries of Western Europe, particularly to France and Germany, from as early as the 5th century AD. Their journeys were greatly facilitated by the extensive network of Roman roads. Following the death of St Columba, in 597 AD, the monastic settlement on Iona, which he established, became a centre of monumental sculpture. Much contact continued with Ireland, country of Columba's birth, and logically it seems probable that Irish masons came to Iona to instruct the brethren in their art.

Of the four eighth-century crosses on Iona, that of St Martin, standing some 21 metres tall, west of the south-west angle of the nave of the abbey church, is the best preserved. The free-standing cross at Kildalton in Islay is also attributed to this period. The charming and intricate patterns of palmate leaves and plait work, which occur so frequently on medieval carvings, indicate an Irish influence based on a classical concept. But the similarity of some of the griffin-like animals to those on stones in Scandinavia may result from the incursions of Viking invaders, who either adopted or introduced these strange effigies of beasts.

The Irish warriors, who came to the aid of the Scots in repelling the Norse invaders, believed that animals accompanied them to Heaven, and the hunting scenes on medieval grave slabs seem to be inspired by this idea. From them we can picture the activities of this age, while the effigies of the knights in the West Highland armour, and of the church dignitaries in their vestments, give a vivid impression of the clothes and accoutrements of their time.

The Irish and Scottish churches of the Celtic era contained communities of Keledei (Cele dei): friends of God. The 'Culdees', as the small groups were called, existed mostly in isolated places until as late as the 14th century.

St Margaret of Scotland, coming as a refugee from England, married Malcolm III, 'Canmore', in 1070, and had much influence over her husband. Renowned as she was for her piety, she encouraged the Church to be organised on a diocesan basis and the Culdee groups were incorporated into a Continental system, governed by the Catholic Church. Subsequently, from that time onwards, trafficking became increasingly frequent between Scotland and Rome. Furthermore, from the 11th to the 15th centuries, many knights from Scotland went on Crusades, firstly to the Holy Land, and then latterly to Spain. The magnificence of the medieval cathedrals of Europe, known to have been a source of inspiration in church building in Scotland, may also have influenced the warriors to perpetuate their being in stone.

Reginald (or Ranald), the second son of Somerled, who inherited the islands of Islay, Jura, Colonsay and Gigha, together with Kintyre and most of Knapdale

OPPOSITE: The Chapel on Inch Kenneth

on the mainland, was a great benefactor to the church. In 1203 he rebuilt St Columba's Abbey on Iona, which had been largely destroyed, and established a brotherhood of Benedictine monks. It is thought that some of the Irish masons, whom he imported to do the work, settled on the island and began to instruct the churchmen, and probably some local men as well, in their art. Subsequently, what is now dubbed the 'Iona School of Sculpture' gradually developed on the island and instructors went from there to teach elsewhere. Outstanding examples of the Iona School of Sculpture can be found within the 13th-century chapel on the island of Inch Kenneth, and also in the burial ground. Also in Lochaline, within the old Parish Church and the graveyard of Cill Choluim Chille, (near to the present Keil Church), which was under the patronage of the Lords of the Isles until their forfeiture, there are beautiful funerary monuments of the Iona School.

The Kintyre School was almost certainly at Saddell Abbey. Another was sited somewhere on Loch Suibhne in Knapdale, close to the Chapel of Kilmory, wherein lie some lovely carved stones. A fourth, known as the Loch Awe School, was probably at Kilmartin. Fine examples of the Loch Awe School are found at Ardchattan Priory on Loch Etive and on Inishail Island in Loch Awe. The craftsmen of this group were itinerant, as is proved by their use of local stone. The masons worked from pattern books, the designs drawn on parchments pierced with small holes, through which some marking substance could be placed on the surface of the stone. The Oronsay School dates from the early 16th century, when following the forfeiture of the Lordship, an Irish master-mason called O'Coull found sanctuary on the island.

The great age of sculpture in the West Highlands and the Isles ended with the Reformation. But stone is resistant to fire, and much of the work of the artists and craftsmen of early historic times has survived to illustrate their skill. Sadly in a book of this size it is possible to describe only a few of the churches, chapels and sculptured stones of this period, which comprise such a treasure of the past.

## IONA ABBEY – CATHEDRAL OF THE ISLES

St Columba had been dead for over 200 years when his island was attacked by Vikings, who sailed from bases in Orkney. The Abbey suffered great damage and many of its treasures, including probably the Book of Kells, were taken for safety to Ireland. Iona was raided three times between 795 and 806, the year in which the whole community was murdered on the strand of Martyr's Bay. Four centuries later the ruined buildings were restored when Reginald, second son of Somerled, established a Benedictine Order of Black Friars in 1202. Traditionally he also founded a nunnery of Augustinian canonesses of which his sister Beatrice became prioress.

St Oran's Chapel, dedicated to a cousin of St Columba, which dates from the 12th century, became the burial place of the Lords of the Isles. It stands near the Rèilig Odhrain, where, according to tradition, lie graves of Scotland's early kings. The Romanesque abbey, built in cruciform shape, stands partly upon the site of St Columba's original foundation. The St Michael Chapel, to the north-east of the chancel, was probably used for worship while work was in progress.

The 13th-century builders used the local grey or black siliceous flagstone, as well as red granite, from the nearby shore of Mull. Most of the roofing was done with thin slabs from the moine schists of the Ross of Mull, but the roofs of the choir and the transepts were covered with Easdale slates. The Abbey was restored in the 15th century under the patronage of the Lords of the Isles. A master mason Donald O'Brolchan, from Donegal, was commissioned, and the mason's marks in the Abbey include an inscription in Lombardic letters: 'Donaldus O (Brolchan F) ecit hoc opus'. (Donald O Brolchan made this work.)

In 1498, following the forfeiture of the Lordship of the Isles, James IV petitioned the Pope to make the Abbey of Colmcille (Iona) the bishop's seat in the Isles. This request being granted, John Campbell was installed as Bishop of the Isles in Iona in 1499. In 1609 Andrew Knox, Bishop of the Isles, having summoned recalcitrant chiefs to Iona, forced them to accept the Statutes which eventually secured their obedience. Repairs were made to the east side of the church in the 1630s, but following the signing of the Covenant in 1638, stones and crosses were thought to be idolatrous, were broken and thrown into the sea. Late in the 17th century Iona was acquired from the MacLeans of Duart by the 9th Earl of Argyll. In 1874 his descendant, the 8th Duke of Argyll, employed the Edinburgh architect R. Rowand Anderson to plan a major renovation. The work was carried out, and in 1899 the Duke made over the building to a body of trustees.

Restoration was renewed, and in 1908 the nave

Iona Abbey

was rebuilt on a design of P. Macgregor Chalmers. The Abbey was then used by the local congregation until, in 1939, the Parish Church was rebuilt. Its future then seemed uncertain. But a man, as dynamic as St Columba, came forward to its rescue. The Reverend George MacLeod (later Lord MacLeod of Fuinary) was at that time minister of Govan Parish Church in Glasgow. The Iona Community, which he founded, included churchmen, divinity students, and some who were unemployed. Inspired by MacLeod's enthusiasm they worked under the direction of the architect Ian G. Lindsay to rebuild the ancient fabric. Work continued during the war, with volunteers instructed by craftsmen. The reredorter was roofed over in 1943, with Canadian timber washed ashore on Mull, and wood for both the roofing and flooring of the refectory was given, in 1947, by Norwegian timber merchants. Materials for the roof of the east range were imported and gifted from New Zealand, and the money for restoring the cloister came mostly from Canada and the USA. Finally, in 1961, the wood for the roof and

the stalls of St Michael's Chapel was bought with money from South Africa. A new west range was completed in 1965, and thus with the help of many nations the great Cathedral of Iona was saved for posterity.

*The Iona School of Monumental Sculpture*

The greatest collection of these outstandingly beautiful carved stones lies within the precincts of Iona Cathedral. Most of the grave slabs, including some transferred from the Rèilig Odhrain, the burial ground of early Scottish kings and chiefs of the Isles, have now been placed in the Abbey Museum to save them from the ravages of the weather. Others stand in the Nunnery Museum and also in the Abbey Church. MacLean's Cross, which is attributed to the late 1400s, stands between the Abbey and the Nunnery, in what is thought to be its original site. The figure of the Crucified Saviour surmounts the shaft which is decorated on both sides with an intricate foliaceous design.

### The Chapel on Inch Kenneth

Outstanding examples of the Iona School can be found in the ruins of the 13th-century chapel and in the churchyard of the small island of Inch Kenneth, which lies to the north of Iona off the west coast of Mull.

### The Old Parish Church of Cill Choluim Chille

The now ruined church, dedicated to St Columba and thought to be of 13th-century date, stands close to the present Keil Church in Lochaline. Originally under the patronage of the Lords of the Isles, it later passed to the crown. The church contains many fine examples of stones of the Iona and Oronsay Schools and the burial ground holds medieval stones as well as some interesting 18th-century tombs.

To the south of the church a disc-headed medieval cross marks the boundary of the religious sanctuary. Built of green schist, the shaft is ornamented with two intertwined plant scrolls, which terminate at the base in a pair of opposed dragon heads, while, on the opposite side, two types of plant scrolls end in a single dragon's head.

Keil Church, the simple white-harled kirk, built on the site of the former parish church of 1799, was designed by Peter MacGregor Chalmers in 1898. The Session House, of 1774, once used as a school, was restored as a museum in 1997. Some of the finest carved grave slabs, now stored there, were taken from outside to prevent erosion by the weather.

### The Cathedral of St Moluag – Lismore

St Columba and St Moluag, both of Irish descent, are said to have been rivals for possession of Lismore. The legend runs that Moluag, approaching the island, saw Columba's birlinn overtaking his own. Placing his hand on the gunwale, he severed his little finger with an axe. Then throwing the finger onto the shore he shouted in Gaelic, 'My flesh and blood have first possession of the island, and I bless it in the name of the Lord.' Columba, furious at being outdone, cursed the rocks, saying they would grow edge-uppermost.

'They will hurt no one to walk on them,' retorted Moluag.

'May you have the alder for your fuel,' yelled Columba.

'Yet it will burn like tinder,' came back Moluag's defiant voice.

True enough, the strata on the eastern side of the island appear to be vertically upturned, but being composed of limestone are easy on the feet. Also alder, known to smoke abominably, burns well on Lismore.

St Moluag's pastoral staff, called the Bachuil Mòr (Great Staff) or the Bachuil Buidhe (Yellow Staff) or the Caman Oir (Golden Shinty Stick), said to be made of blackthorn, is 2 feet 9 inches (0.79m) high. Once encased in metal and probably studded with jewels, it was entrusted to a family who became almoners to Lismore Cathedral and Barons of Bachuil. During the late 17th and early 18th centuries many of the family changed their names from MacDhunsleibhe or MacLea to Livingstone. Neil Livingstone, Baron of Bachuil, is custodian of the pastoral staff today. All traces of the monastery, traditionally founded in the 6th century by St Moluag, a contemporary of St Columba, have vanished, but c1189 a church, consisting of a nave and a choir, was built as the cathedral of the diocese of Argyll. In 1456 the cathedral withstood attack when the island was laid to waste by the MacDonalds of the Isles (see pp. 40–41). Following the Reformation, the nave of the Cathedral became ruinous, but the choir was rebuilt as the parish church which remains in use today. The buttresses against the south wall are part of the original building.

### Ardchattan Priory

The Priory of Ardchattan is believed to have been built, c1230, by Duncan MacDougall of Argyll (d.1247). Duncan, who was himself the grandson of Somerled, was the grandfather of Alexander of Argyll. The Priory, which stands in a sunny sheltered site on the north shore of Loch Etive, was a house of the strict Vallis-caulian Order. Outlines of the monk's fishponds can still be traced in the garden. The story runs that a prior fell in love with one of the sisters of a now long-lost nunnery on the island, which lies just off Muckairn on the other side of Loch Etive. Surprised by the visit of a bishop, he hid her below the floor in the sacristy where, supposedly forgotten, she died. In 1309, following his conquest of Argyll, King Robert the Bruce summoned the local chiefs to attend a Council at Ardchattan. The business was conducted in Gaelic, translated for the King to understand (see p. 34).

Little remains of the original structure, but most

of the building of the 15th and early 16th centuries survives, at least in part. Medieval grave slabs, within the ruins, are those of West Highland warriors. A grave slab of 18th-century date is that of Colin Campbell of Glenure, known locally as 'The Red Fox' (see p. 82). The stone was purposely left unmarked for fear of desecration at the time. However, in the part of the burial ground designated to the Campbells of Glenure, three stones lie together of which the centre one, which is cracked, is thought to be that of Colin, victim of an assassin whose name has never been revealed.

Following the Reformation the priory became the property of Alexander Campbell, formerly its commendatory prior. His descendant Mrs Sara Troughton, daughter of the late Lieutenant Colonel R.MT. Campbell-Preston, remains in ownership today. The monks of the 13th–16th centuries, needing herbs for medicinal purposes, probably began the garden.

The garden is open daily from April until October.

Ardchattan Priory

## Saddell Abbey

Saddell Abbey, traditionally founded by Somerled, who is said to be buried there, was probably finished by his son Donald, patronymic founder of the clan. The original church, of cruciform shape, dating from the latter half of the 12th century, contained a nave and a choir, with transepts to the north and south. A cloister, on the south side, was also surrounded by buildings. The brethren were Cistercians, known as the white or grey friars because of their clothing.

Traditionally, in 1263, when the great fleet of Haakon, King of Norway, lay off the island of Gigha, the Abbot of Saddell, asking for protection, was granted it in writing by the Norwegian King. Later, in 1306, King Robert the Bruce, at that time a hunted man, is thought to have landed at Port Righ, some four miles north of Saddell. Reputedly Angus MacDonald (son of MacDonald of the Isles) then organised his escape by sea to Rathlin Island (see p. 33).

Circa 1507, on the suggestion of James IV, the Abbey became part of the bishopric of Argyll. The lands of Saddell were converted into a barony and David Hamilton, Bishop of Argyll, built the old castle of Saddell on a nearby site. Early in the 1770s, much of the stone of the Abbey was taken for building the new castle and for its offices and stables.

The finest of the sculptured grave slabs at Saddell are now housed within a shelter by the entrance to

Sculptured slabs at Saddell Abbey

the Abbey grounds. Mostly of the Kintyre School (and probably carved on the premises), they present an amazingly accurate picture of the armour and weaponry of the West Highland warriors until late medieval times. Typically they wear the conical bascinets and the aketons, the padded coats, and carry both sword and spear. Those depicting galleys may indicate family connections with the MacDonalds of the Isles. Tombstones of ecclesiastics show them robed in their vestments, with a chalice to indicate their calling.

### The Pre-Reformation Chapels of the Lordship of the Isles

Many of these simple chapels, dating in some cases from as early as the 12th century, are found within the area of the Lordship, which lay in Knapdale and Kintyre. Those in Kintyre include:

### Kilchousland Old Parish Church

Standing above cliffs on the edge of the sea about 3.5 km north-east of Campbeltown, the church dates back to the 12th century. It was rebuilt during the 16th century, and the gravestones in the churchyard include medieval slabs and also two 18th-century headstones, depicting a farmer and his plough-team, which stand against the church wall.

### The Old Parish Church, Kilkivan

This church lies within its churchyard, about 180m south of the main Campbeltown–Machrihanish road, adjacent to a sand quarry. Six of the eight late medieval West Highland grave slabs at the east end of the ruined church are attributed to the Kintyre School. Two depict hunting scenes of stags pursued by hounds.

### The Old Parish Church of Kilchenzie

The 12th-century church surmounts a knoll on the south side of the main Tarbert–Campbeltown road, about 6 km north-west of the latter. Medieval stones of the Kintyre School, within the ruined church, include one with the inscription 'HIC JACET KATE-RINA FILIA NEIL' ('Here lies Katherine, daughter of Neil', presumably one of a local family of MacNeils). A group of creatures, two birds, an otter and a salmon, and beasts with ornamental tails are depicted on the end of the stone.

### St Columba's Church, Southend

The oldest part of the building, at the east end, is attributed to the 13th century. Medieval tombstones, within the church and outside, are ascribed to the Kintyre School. Traditionally, St Columba preached to the local people on the rocky knoll above the church where 'St Columba's Footsteps' are carved upon flat rock. They are in fact two right feet, between which the figures 564 have been rudely incised. More factually it is known that although the southern one may be a thousand years old, the other was the work of a local stonemason no earlier than 1856. The significance of the footprint is that it proves that this, like Dunadd and Dunollie, was an inauguration site. Nearby St Columba's Well, long venerated by pagan people on account of its supposedly miraculous water, later became a place of worship for Christians.

Places change with time. The burial ground was divided between the original Highlanders and the Lowland farmers from Ayrshire. Most were settled here by the Marquess of Argyll, after Kintyre was devastated by the plague brought over by the government army, sent from Edinburgh to defeat Alasdair MacColla MacDonald in 1647 (see p. 72).

### Kilbrannan Chapel – Skipness

The chapel, near the shore of Skipness Bay, is believed to have been built during the late 13th century to replace an earlier one in Skipness Castle. Sculptured stones of unusually beautiful design are preserved within boxes, constructed by Historic Scotland.

### Chapels of Knapdale

### The Chapel of St Charmaig, Keills

The site of the chapel on a hillside, where wild thyme grows amongst the rocks, about 4 miles (6.4km) south-west of the village of Tayvallich, has been sacred since the 8th century. Traces of an earlier building, and of graves cut in the rocks, have been found by archaeologists. The chapel is of 13th-century date, the round-headed rear arch of the east window being typical of the style of building of the 12th and early 13th centuries. Three of the four windows, placed round the east end, throw light onto the altar, and the three recesses in the east wall were used to hold

Kilbrannan Chapel, Skipness

the Holy vestments. The modern door in the north wall replaced an earlier entrance.

The chapel became ruinous after the Reformation and was used simply as a burial enclosure until, in 1972, it was placed in the guardianship of the Secretary of State for Scotland by Mr W.P. Neill. The restoration, undertaken after 1972, included the modern roofing and the placing within the chapel of most of the historic monuments.

Outside in the graveyard stands the early Christian Cross, which may be of ninth-century date. Its central boss is a bird's nest containing three eggs, which symbolise the Holy Trinity. The later grave slabs of the 14th–16th centuries, within the chapel, contain fine examples of the skill of the masons of the Iona, the Loch Awe and, in particular, the local Loch Suibhne (Loch Sween) Schools of Monumental Sculpture.

A sculptured slab on top of a box tomb, in the north-east corner, with carvings which include a harp and its tuning key, is attributed to the Loch Suibhne School. Another, at the opposite end, bearing a claymore, a hunting scene and a galley, carries a Latin inscription meaning 'Here lies Torquil, son of Malcolm, son of Neil'. This is thought to commemorate the grandson of Neil, keeper of Castle Suibhne, during the mid-16th century.

## The Chapel of Kilmory Knap

This lovely chapel, dedicated to the Virgin Mary, stands on close-cropped turf, above the east shore of Loch Suibhne (Loch Sween) some 10 miles (15km) south of the village of Achnamara. It bears close resemblance to St Charmaig at Keills, in that the windows were placed in the east wall, so that light would fall on the Psalter while the priests were celebrating mass.

The chapel – an ancient monument – is now roofed to hold what is probably the finest collection of medieval grave slabs in the whole of the West Highlands. Some of the oldest stones (on the left as you enter the door) may even be of eighth-century date. Medieval slabs bearing swords are those of warrior knights, and others depicting axes, blacksmith's tools and shears are probably those of artisans.

The MacMillan Cross (which bears great similarity to the MacLean Cross on Iona) dates from the late 15th century. The cross head, on the front, shows the Crucifixion above a sword, and the back depicts a hunting scene, with a huntsman, his dogs and a deer. An inscription in Lombardic capitals shows it to be the monument of Alexander MacMillan, son-in-law of a previous MacNeil Captain from whom he received nearby lands (see p. 15). A rock by the sea bears words

Keills Cross, St Charmaig Chapel

The MacMillan Cross, Kilmory Knap

to the effect that 'MacMillan's right shall stand while waves beat on this rock'. The family remained in charge of Castle Suibhne until the latter half of the 15th century.

## The Chapel on Eilean Mor

Eilean Mor is the largest and most westerly of the islands known as 'the MacCormac Isles', which lie in the Sound of Jura at the mouth of Loch Suibhne. Carvings within a cave are of early Christian date. The ruined chapel upon it, dating originally from the 13th century, is known to have been repaired in the middle of the 14th century by John, Lord of the Isles. Outstanding amongst the monuments is the shaft of a cross. One side is badly worn, but the other shows a monster, which seems to be swallowing a snake. Below it a hooded horseman sits astride his steed, while at the foot of the shaft two bird-headed monsters seem locked in a deadly embrace.

## THE CHURCHES AND CHAPELS OF ISLAY

### The Old Parish Church of Kildalton

The ruined church stands within its churchyard amongst low-lying hills some nine miles (13.5 km) north-east of Port Ellen in the south-east end of Islay. Dating from the late 12th or early 13th century, the building, although roofless, is otherwise almost complete. The Chancel stands at the east end of the church but the two original doorways, held by draw-bars, are almost opposite to each other in the north and south walls of the adjoining nave.

The name Kildalton is derived from the Gaelic Cill Dalton, meaning 'church of the foster child or follower', and Kildalton was the parish church, under the patronage of the Bishops of the Isles, until late in the 17th century. It then became ruinous but was skilfully renovated by the Islay Historic Works Group in 1973–74.

## *The Kildalton Cross*

This exceptional example of an early Christian ringed cross stands just to the north of the chancel. It dates from the second half of the 8th century and is carved from the local grey-green epidiorite, but its strong resemblance to the group of free-standing crosses on Iona suggests it to be the work of a mason of that school. The design on the west side is contrived around bosses and contains both serpents and lions. On the east face, a panel at the top of the shaft depicts the Virgin and Child, with angels on either side holding their wings above their heads. The left arm of the cross shows Cain murdering Abel with the jaw bone of an ass (or, as has been otherwise suggested, David rending the jaws of the lion), while on the right arm we see Abraham offering Isaac in sacrifice. The shaft of the cross contains an intricate trumpet design, which reaches to the foot of the stone. It seems almost miraculous that a monument of such artistry and magnificence has survived, almost unimpaired, in a remote part of Islay, for over 1,200 years.

### The Chapel of Kilnave – Islay

The name of this chapel comes from the Gaelic Cill Naoimh, meaning the cell of the saint, but standing as it does on the west coast of Loch Gruinard, within sight of a stretch of sea notoriously treacherous to shipping, it is truly a sailor's haven. The building which, although roofless, is still largely intact, is of 13th–14th century date. Traditionally it was burned when survivors from the battle of Traigh Gruineard, between the MacDonalds and the MacLeans of Duart, on the strand of the bay below, tried to find sanctuary within the walls (see pp. 63–64).

### The Kilnave Cross

The early Christian Cross in the burial ground is carved from a slab of local flagstone. It was probably made in the second half of the 8th century, but through constant exposure to wind and rain it has become very badly worn. Unlike the Kildalton Cross of the same period, it is ringless, and the design is less elaborate. But, in its very simplicity, this ancient cross by the ocean exemplifies the true Christian faith.

### The Old Parish Church of Kilchoman

Two very ancient cross slabs in the churchyard suggest that the present church, of the early-19th century (now unused), replaced an earlier building of some considerable importance.

The Chapel of Kilnave, Islay

The Kilchoman Cross

## The Kilchoman Cross

A later medieval cross is attributed to the Iona School. The carving on the front displays the Crucifixion, and the back is decorated with an intricate Celtic design of circles above a pattern of foliage rising from the tails of animals. The Cross bears a Latin inscription, which translates, 'This is the cross by Thomas, son of Patrick, doctor', making it probable that it commemorates one of the Beatons, physicians of the Lords of the Isles, who held land in this locality. Sir James MacDonald, when nearly fatally wounded at the battle of Traigh Gruineard in 1598 (see pp. 63–64) was saved by the skill of one of the family. Other stones within the churchyard include many of medieval date. Also here are graves of those drowned in shipwrecks off the dangerous coast.

### The Round Church, Bowmore

The Church was built by Donald Campbell of Islay, 'Donald the Younger', in 1767 for the cost of £700. The architect is unknown, but its great resemblance to a slightly smaller church, built by William Adam at Hamilton in 1732, suggests that the idea came from plans for a new church at Inveraray, drawn up by William Adam and his son John.

The building has two storeys, the U-shaped gallery on the first floor being supported by wooden pillars from below. The round-headed main door, with its fanlight, stands in the north wall and above it the tower rises in four stages to end in a stone cupola. Two enclosed staircases lead to the gallery from doors on the east and west sides. The interior was remodelled at the end of the Victorian era, when pews replaced the box seats. Within the porch, a white marble monument commemorates Walter Campbell of Shawfield who died in 1816.

The Reverend Donald Caskie, famous in the last world war as the Tartan Pimpernel for his rescue of allied soldiers and airmen from German-occupied France, was born in a farm near Bowmore. His decorations, the British OBE and the French OCF, are held in a niche in the south-facing wall of the church.

### Oronsay Priory

Oronsay, to the south-west of Colonsay, can be reached across a causeway at low tide. Halfway across stands the now much worn Sanctuary Cross, where poor Malcolm MacDuffie, fleeing from pursuing MacDonalds, thought, alas mistakenly, that he had found safety from pursuit (see p. 67). Today, on reaching Oronsay, the visitor must watch the time, for it is

The Round Church, Bowmore

easy to become entranced and then stranded by the inrush of the swift running tide.

Oronsay, traditionally the site of a monastery in the 6th century, has long been a place of veneration. The Priory, dedicated to St Columba, was founded by John I (Good John of Islay) *c*1325. The lancet windows are almost identical to those of the old parish Church of Kildalton on Islay, and both were given by him to the Church in gratitude for the Bill of Divorce which permitted his second marriage to the Princess Margaret, daughter of Robert II. All that remains now of the early building are parts of the east range, the greater part of the existing church, and the sanctuary, being of late-14th and early-15th-century date.

The office of Prior was held, almost continuously, by relations of the Chiefs of the MacDuffies (or MacPhees), hereditary holders of Colonsay and Oronsay from before recorded time, and vassals of the MacDonalds of Islay after Somerled's conquest of the Isles. The chapel, called the MacDuffies' Aisle, was added in the 16th century on the south side of the choir. Following the forfeiture of the Lordship of the Isles in 1493, the Abbey of Iona, then the nucleus of civilisation in the Western Highlands, deteriorated from lack of sponsorship. Fortunately, the MacDuffies of Oronsay invited the Irish master-mason, Mael-Sechlainn O Cuinn,

Oronsay Priory

who had trained in Iona, to come to Oronsay to build the cloister arcade and to found the Oronsay School of Monumental Sculpture.

Many of the finest carvings of the first half of the 16th century have survived within the Priory, but following the Reformation of 1560, this great centre of art was abandoned to become ruinous. Some restoration was made in 1883 and the Prior's House, which contains some of the finest carvings, was rebuilt in 1927.

*The Sculptured Stones of Oronsay*

The RCAHMS (Argyll Vol. 5) lists 12 exceptionally fine examples of the Iona School dating from the 14th-15th centuries. Amongst the best of the Oronsay School is the grave slab erected to Murdoch, or Murchudus MacDuffie, who died in 1539. Erected by his sister Mariota MacLean, it is thought to be carved by O Cuinn. The design is centred around a claymore, surmounted by a scene of deer-hunting hounds. Beneath them, a foliate pattern descends from tails of a lion and a griffin down either side of the sword, to a galley carrying full sail. Other slabs include the gravestone of Sir Donald MacDuffie, Prior of Oronsay, in all his ecclesiastical regalia, and those of West Highland warriors, with the armour and weaponry of the time.

The Oronsay Cross

The outstandingly beautiful cross, which stands in the churchyard just north of the Priory, is proved by an inscription on the base to be the work of O Cuinn. It commemorates Colin, or Malcolm MacDuffie, who was chief of his clan at the end of the 15th century, with Lombardic capitals on the font that read: 'HEC EST CR/UX COLINI F/ILLI CHRISTI/NI M(EIC)DUFACI'. ('This is the cross of Colinus (Malcolm Gille-Colium) son of Christinus MacDuffie.') This side of the cross is carved with a figure of the Crucified Saviour above a design of roundels, which spring from the tails of strange beasts. A similar motif on the reverse side surmounts a foliated cross, while the cross-head is filled with a circular design based on an eight-petalled flower. Thus, after nearly 500 years, a chief is remembered by the work of the sculptor who found sanctuary within his isle.

Oronsay Priory, sculptured slabs

The Oronsay Cross

## CHURCHES ON THE MAINLAND OF ARGYLL

*Kilneuair – Church of the Yews, South Lochaweside*

The B840 along Lochaweside reaches a marked foot-path to Lochfyneside (r.h. side) about two miles from Ford. This is a former drove road leading over the hill to Loch Fyne. A short way up the track, on the left, lie the ruins of Kilneuair Church; the yews that gave the church its name have long disappeared (NM889 037 sheet 15). A charming tradition persists that the church was built from stones quarried and dressed at Killevin on Lochfyneside, a place about 12 miles distant. The local people, passing the stones from hand to hand down the length of a human chain, thus prevented the sacred site from being dese-crated by the noise of hammering.

More factually it is known that the church, dedi-cated to St Columba, was once the Parish Church of Glassary and that, because of its prime position, a market was held at its gates. The earliest part of the building, at the east end of the chancel, dates from the 13th century. Much of the south wall was rebuilt sometime during the 16th century, by the Scrymgeour lords of Glassary, of the nearby castle of Fincharn, who were patrons of the parish. Kilneuair was replaced as the parish church by that of Kilmichael Glassary during the 16th century (see p. 32).

Disused, it became neglected and the font, broken and used as a cattle trough, was only recently restored. The building, now roofless, has two south-facing doors. Beyond them the churchyard contains some fine examples of grave slabs of the Loch Awe School. One, depicting a design of foliage and plaited cords, with a pair of shears above, has been superimposed with a Latin cross. The claim by two American authors that this proves it to be the grave of a Knight Templar cannot be substantiated.

It is however the source of a local legend. Tradi-tionally a tailor once accepted a wager to stay in the church through the night. He sat cross-legged, stitching away with diligence, until the Devil emerged. Then throwing his scissors in terror, he made a bolt for the door where the Devil, just failing to grab him, left fingerprints embedded by the lintel. The marks, now barely discernible to the left of the western door, may be a fossilised footprint.

A ruined oratory in the churchyard is of 18th-century date.

Kilmartin Parish Church

## Kilmartin Parish Church

The Parish Church of Kilmartin, on high ground on the east side of Kilmartin Glen, looks down upon the wide green strath where burial cairns and standing stones prove ancient habitation. The present church, rectangular in shape and adjoined to a western tower, was built in 1835, to replace an earlier building, on the plans of J. Gordon Davis.

Within the church the architect achieved maximum light by the placing of a window above each of the four arcades, which form a distinctive feature on either side of the aisle. Renovations were carried out in 1900, when the fine panelled ceiling was installed.A 16th-century cross, moved inside the church for protection, is one of the treasures of the Highlands. The work of an unknown sculptor, it depicts the pathos and the suffering of the Crucifixion with its pure simplicity of design.

The former manse, built in 1789, became Kilmartin House Museum, which opened in May 1997. It contains an audio-visual display and museum as well as a café and a bookshop. The museum houses some of the treasures that have been excavated from important local sites and monuments. Others are on loan from the National Museum of Scotland, Glasgow Museums and the British Museum.

Survey work in Kilmartin Glen has resulted in the discovery of nearly 800 historic and prehistoric monuments within a six-mile radius of Kilmartin village. With its standing stones, burial cairns, rock art, forts, duns and carved stones it is one of the richest archaeological landscapes in Scotland. Mid Argyll has the densest concentration of cup and ring marked rocks in the British Isles (see Achnabreck p. 4).

A cairn cemetery was used for burials during both the Neolithic and Bronze Ages (c6000BC–c2600BC). There is a henge monument at Ballymeanoch (the middle town) as well as a stone circle. Other circles and alignments are at Templewood,

Lady Glassary, Achnasheloch, Nether Largie and Ballymeanoch. During the Bronze Age, the Glen saw an intensive period of monumental construction. The density and type of 'grave goods' such as jet necklaces and pottery vessels found within indicate the importance of the area in this period. Comparable archaeological remains are found around Stonehenge on Salisbury Plain, in Wiltshire.

All the evidence of the Neolithic and Bronze Age occupation of the Glen is based on funerary monuments. The first millennium, however, was a time of dramatic change. Iron was used in duns, forts and crannogs (fortified settlements on islands in lochs) where people actually lived. Dunadd, the hill at the foot of the glen, where early Scots kings were crowned, has already been described in the first part of this book.

The first Christian monuments in the area date from around the 6th century. It seems that by the time St Columba came to Iona in 563 AD, most people in Argyll had been converted to Christianity. Some early crosses are engraved with both Christian and pagan symbols, suggesting a combining of old religions with the new. A recent find only a few miles from Kilmartin – the Kilbride cross slab – reveals possible links with the Iona School of Monumental Carving of ninth-century date.

Many other Christian carved stones have been found in the locality. Kilmartin Parish Church itself, standing next to the museum, contains an exceptional collection of late medieval grave slabs. Many of the magnificent West Highland warriors, depicted with their weapons of war, are the work of the Loch Awe School of itinerant masons of the 14th and 15th centuries. The theory put forward by two American authors that they marked the graves of Knights Templar bears no authenticity to date.

*The Old Parish Church, Kilmarie, Craignish*

The ruins of the church dedicated to St Maelrubha of Applecross stand upon a rise above the west shore of Loch Craignish (a short way from Craignish Castle) overlooking the sea. The church, which is believed to date from the 13th century, although largely roofless, survives as a near-perfect shell. The names of the parsons of Craignish are recorded from 1395. Kilmarie Church seems to have been abandoned when a new church (possibly on the site of the present one) was built in the village of Ardfern in 1608.

Medieval carved warrior, Kilmarie, Craignish

Kilmarie Church was restored by the Craignish estate in the 19th century and later saved by local people, at the instigation of the Natural History and Antiquarian Association of Mid Argyll, in 1974. The society supervised the transfer of some of the finest stones from the churchyard to within the church. They include two early Christian crosses and many fine examples of medieval grave slabs, mostly of the Loch Awe School. Four tomb chests of 16th-century date (two against the south and two against the north walls) are of special interest. Deer chased by hounds are depicted as well as intriguing foliate designs.[33]

Sailing from Craignish, St Maelrubha reached Kilmelfort, at the head of Loch Melfort, where he is said to have founded a chapel. From there he went overland to Kilmore and on to Loch Etive. He built a chapel at Kilmarrow (now Kilvarie) and Eilean an t-Sagairt, the priest's island on the Black Loch, just west of Connell, is said to have been the site of his cell. Nearby, at Dunstaffnage Castle, the now ruined chapel is called Kilmorrie. It is from here that Maelrubha is said to have set off to travel beyond the mountains of Drumalban, the western boundary of the Picts.[34]

*The Pre-Reformation Chapel on Inishail Island, Loch Awe*

Inishail, the Holy Island in Loch Awe, was a place of worship from very early days. Like so many others in the West Highlands, its origins spring from myth. It is dedicated to St Findoca, one of nine sisters, who, following her father's death, was given shelter by a Pictish ruler called Garnait who held sway in Perthshire from 706 to 729 AD. Heading west, first by boat up Loch Tay, then over the time-trodden track through Glen Dochart and Strathfillan to Tyndrum, she must then have come down Glen Lochy into Glen Orchy, to find her way to Loch Awe.

The first dwelling on Inishail Island is thought to have been a nunnery. St Columba knew of it as St Adomnan, his biographer records. The nuns, who likewise probably came from Ireland, were renowned for 'the sanctity of their lives and the purity of their manners'. A legend persists that it was they who first planted daffodils and lent lilies from their native land, which shine like stars against black water in the spring sunlight every year. The peaceful atmosphere of the island seems resonant with the spirit of these brave, devoted women who created a haven of charity in a country ravaged by fighting and where wolves howled eerily at night. The cross-decorated slab, originally in the churchyard but now placed upright within the chapel's ruined shell, which dates from the 9th century, proves Christian occupation at that time.

Pilgrims came up Glen Aray, the Gaelic name for Glen of Worship, until, at the watershed, they saw the island before them lying beneath the mighty mountain of Cruachan, on still days mirrored in Loch Awe. Overjoyed, they knelt to pray in thankfulness by a rock (no longer identifiable) called the Kneeling Stone. Then, descending to the south shore of the loch, they were ferried to the island, target of so many weary miles.

The first recorded mention of the church is in 1257 when Ath, son of Malcolm MacNachtan, granted the teinds, or tithes, of 'the church of St Findoca of Inchealt to the Augustinian canons of Inchaffray Abbey'. It seems to have been at about that time that the church on Inishail became a monastery. The monk's fish ponds, overgrown with moss, can still clearly be seen.

Amongst carved stones of the medieval period in the churchyard is a parallel-sided slab, taken to have been an altar frontal. It shows a crucifix flanked by two figures, one of which holds a chalice and the other a cup to catch the blood dripping from the wounds. To the left are two men-at-arms. Both carry swords and spears, while the one on the extreme left also has an axe. This is taken to mean that he was a McWhannel (in Gaelic McIlchonnel, son of Connel) and therefore one of the hereditary boat builders of the Earls of Argyll. To the right a heraldic group of two or more armed men support a crown above a shield charged with a galley with furled sail.

The island was later held by MacArthurs of Tirrevadich until, in the mid 16th century, they were driven out by Campbells of Inverawe. A fragment of ancient paper in the Duke of Argyll's charter chest in Inveraray proves the pardon of the Campbells of Inverawe for the 'drowning of Clan Arthur', presumably in a last-ditch stand.

The now ruined chapel remained the Parish Church, it being easier to travel by water than road, until 1736. Afterwards it is said to have been taken, stone by stone, to be re-erected on the shore, near Cladich, a short way to the west of the island of Inishail. An aunt of the poet Samuel Taylor Coleridge,

touring the Highlands in her coach in the early 1800s, described the Sunday service. The church was full of healthy-looking country people, the women wrapped in shawls. Many had come in boats, drawn up on the nearby shore.

## Dalmally Church, The Parish Church of Glenorchy

The church stands upon Eilean a Portair (Isle of the Ferryman), which, as its name implies, was originally an island. Traditionally a man with a grey horse waited by a shallow stretch of the river near the bridge below the church. The horse, having carried people across, returned at its owner's whistle. Presumably both the horse and the old man were made redundant when the three-arch bridge, which carries the old road from Bonawe via Stronmichan to Dalmally, across the River Orchy, was constructed by the contractor, who had already built Bridge of Awe, in 1780.[35]

Traditionally three of the old Scottish Kings are buried near to the church door and St Conan, to whom it is dedicated – a disciple of Columba – is believed to have come here in the 7th century on a mission to convert the Picts. The church is first mentioned in the 14th century as a burial place of the MacGregors, then holders of Glenorchy and Glenstrae. A large number of human bones, discovered during recent renovations below the floor of the present church, are believed to be those of MacGregors who died, either in battle, or else fell victims of a plague.

In 1615 the church was rebuilt by Sir Duncan Campbell, 7th of Glenorchy, for the cost of £1,000 Scots. In 1807, his descendant, the 4th Earl of Breadalbane, commissioned a new building, the architect being James Elliot of Edinburgh, and the contractor Allan Johnston. The church is constructed in the unusual form of a buttressed octagon, attached to a square tower, within which a wooden stair leads up to a small vestry and the gallery. Most of the existing furniture, the pulpit, and the stained-glass window date from extensive remodelling carried out in 1898.

In 1985 the fabric was declared unsafe, and in 1988 the huge task of restoration was commenced. Grants were obtained, but the enormous cost, surpassing £220,000, was largely met by the small congregation, which, headed by the Rev. W.T. Hogg and the Glenorchy Historical Association, worked with tireless determination to complete the undertaking of renovating this historic church.

## The Sculptured Stones

The 14th and 15th century stones in the churchyard are all of the Loch Awe School. One on the north-west side has a particularly lovely foliate design and others bear effigies of warriors. Most of these were probably MacGregors, but many commemorate Fletchers, hereditary arrow makers of the MacGregors, and MacNabs, who were hereditary armourers to the Campbells of Glenorchy, as well as other local families.

A headstone bearing a cherub's head and wings is that of the Rev. John MacVean, minister of Clachan Dysart (the old name for Dalmally) who died in 1794. Another, erected by John MacNab in memory of his father, Alexander MacNab of Barran (a now ruined township east of Dalmally) who died in 1814, bears a shield with his coat of arms on its reverse.

## St Conan's Kirk, Loch Awe

This unique church, in its lovely position on the north shore of Loch Awe, was the inspiration and the life's work of a most unusual man. Walter Douglas Campbell, a younger brother of the 1st Lord Blythswood, bought the nearby island of Innischonan from the Marquess of Breadalbane and began by building a small church, on the site of the present building, in 1881. He embarked on the enlargement in 1907, but died before it was finished. Nonetheless his sister, and subsequently trustees, completed the work he had begun.

Campbell was his own architect and reputedly tried to include examples of all types of ecclesiastical architecture in his church. He was also a skilled crafts-man and he himself carved the organ screen in the nave. The window above is painted by his sister Helen. All the work was done locally, the very stones of the building being split and shaped from boulders which were rolled down the slopes of Cruachan. The lead-work, including the gargoyles of a dog chasing two hares, was done by William Bonnington.

The form of the church includes a transept, a chancel and three small chapels. One is dedicated to King Robert the Bruce, who conquered the MacDougalls in the nearby Pass of Brander in 1309.

An ossuary below his effigy holds a fragment of his bone. St Conan's Kirk is a memorial to a man who, inspired by an idyllic concept, created a beautiful and most exceptional church.

## A Church of the 20th Century – St Columba's Cathedral, Oban

The Roman Catholic Cathedral of Oban resulted from the determination of the Right Reverend Donald Martin, who, on becoming Bishop of Argyll and the Isles in 1919, decided that a new church must be built to replace the existing one, made of corrugated iron. To this purpose he campaigned tirelessly, travelling as far as America to raise funds. Then finally, on 14 September 1932, he laid the foundation stone.

The architect was Sir Giles Gilbert-Scott, foremost exponent of the modern Gothic style in which the cathedral is designed. The contractors were Messrs D. and J. MacDougall of Oban, who used both blue granite from Kentallen near Glencoe, and pink granite from Aberdeenshire in the construction of the walls. The work progressed slowly during the Second World War, and the great tower was finished only in 1953. The two large bells, called 'Kenneth' and 'Brendan', were blessed by Bishop Kenneth Grant (himself an ex-prisoner of war) in 1959.

A picture within the cathedral, over the main door, shows St Columba sailing in his coracle on Loch Ness while pagan priests defy him from the safety of the shore. The carving of the panels on the front of the High Altar are the work of Donald Gilbert FRBS. One of them shows St Columba's confrontation with Brude, King of the Picts, near Inverness, and another his meeting with St Mungo (or St Kentigern), the patron saint of Glasgow. In this the two are exchanging crosiers in token of the reconciliation achieved between the Celts of Dal Riata and the Britons of Strathclyde.

The Cathedral stands above the sea at the north-west end of the town, from where one can see the islands beyond the Firth of Lorn. St Columba may have come here to spread the word of God, and the church on the edge of the ocean, which is dedicated to his name, is a fitting memorial to this great evangelist of the past.

# CHAPTER 4: Clans and Conflict

## ARREST AND EXECUTION OF JOHN MACDONALD OF DUNYVAIG AND HIS SONS

On 18 August 1493, King James IV held a court at Dunstaffnage Castle on Loch Etive. Before coming to Argyll he had learned some Gaelic so that he could communicate, at least to some extent, with those he met. He knighted several men of importance in the hopes of achieving their obedience. Amongst them were two of the chiefs of the MacDonalds, namely Alexander of Lochalsh, who had been so recently rebellious, and John of Dunyvaig.

But despite the honour shown to them, the MacDonalds remained so openly hostile that the King decided that a show of strength at sea, so long the sphere of their monopoly, was the only way to impress them. Accordingly, in the spring of 1494, he sailed from Dumbarton with a strong naval force, commanded by Sir Andrew Wood, and came ashore at Tarbert at the north-east end of Kintyre. He returned in July, and this time sailed from Tarbert down to the Mull of Kintyre. There he seized the castle of Dunaverty, the duthus (inheritance land) on the mainland of the MacDonalds of Dunyvaig. He installed a garrison, but hardly had he put back to sea than a party of the MacDonalds, led by their chief, John MacDonald of Dunyvaig and his son John Catanach, were storming and retaking the castle. The King was forced to watch helplessly while his newly installed governor was hanged over the ramparts. Returning to Edinburgh he summoned John of Dunyvaig and his sons to court. Predictably they failed to appear and the King, who was aware of a disagreement between them and the MacIains of Ardnamurchan, exploited their known enmity.

John MacIain of Ardnamurchan had quarrelled with the MacDonalds of Dunyvaig over possession of land in Sunart. Now on the King's instruction he sailed to Islay where, apparently at Finlaggan, he arrested John of Dunyvaig and his four eldest sons and took them to Edinburgh in chains. There, on a charge of treachery, they were hanged on the Borough-muir outside the city on newly constructed gallows. The family was thus almost exterminated, but two little boys, the youngest of John's sons, who had been taken to Ireland for safety, survived.

James IV made several more visits to Argyll and the Isles, and in 1498 he commissioned Archibald, 2nd Earl of Argyll, as his lieutenant over the whole of the former Lordship of the Isles and hereditary governor of the Royal Castle of Tarbert.

## SUMMARY OF MAIN EVENTS 1513–1545

*Sir Donald MacDonald (Donald Gallda) of Lochalch*

Alexander MacDonald of Dunyvaig
Sir John Campbell of Calder
Rebellions of Donald Dubh

James IV was killed at the Battle of Flodden in 1513 and Archibald, 2nd Earl of Argyll, was among the many Scotsmen who fell fighting by his side. One who survived the battle was Sir Donald MacDonald of Lochalsh, known as 'Donald Gallda' (Donald the Lowlander), who proclaimed himself Lord of the Isles.

First he made a punitive raid on Ardnamurchan, where he burned the castle of Mingary to the ground in revenge for MacIain's betrayal of John of Dunyvaig and his sons. Then joined by John's son Alexander, the oldest of the two little boys who had been sent to Ireland for safety, he again raided Ardnamurchan where, in a fierce battle near Kilchoan, they killed MacIain and two of his sons. Colin, 3rd Earl of Argyll, was ordered 'to persew Donald of the Isles and expel him', but before he could take action, Donald died in the Treshnish Isles.

### Alexander MacDonald of Dunyvaig

Subsequently Alexander of Dunyvaig was pardoned and his lands in Islay and Kintyre were restored to him on a five-year lease, conditional to his making a Bond of Gossipry (by which a lesser chief swore loyalty to a greater) with John Campbell of Calder. This is the first indication that this third son of the second Earl of Argyll, who had married the Calder heiress, was determined to acquire the MacDonald lands by any possible means.

### Sir John Campbell of Calder

James V, on attaining his majority in 1528, cancelled all grants of land made during his minority, and Calder, in proof of his intentions, immediately raided Colonsay. Alexander of Dunyvaig, incensed by this injustice, came out in open rebellion, and with the MacLeans of Duart and the MacDonalds of Largie, raided the Campbell lands of Rosneath and Craignish. The Campbells in retaliation laid waste to the MacLean lands of Morvern, and moved on to Coll and Tiree. Calder then approached the Scottish Counsel with the suggestion that a peace-keeping force from the Lowlands be placed under his brother's command.

But James V, aware of the Campbells' ambitions, instead sent a herald to Islay to order Alexander of Dunyvaig to disband his men and to present himself at court to seek a pardon. Alexander obeyed the summons and at Stirling, on 7 June 1531, was granted royal clemency.

In 1540 the King made a great naval expedition round the coast of his kingdom with a fleet of twelve ships, and a force of about 1,500 men. Having rounded the north of Scotland he sailed down to the Western Isles where he took Hector, son of MacLean of Duart, and James, heir to Alexander MacDonald of Dunyvaig, aboard as hostages for their father's obedience. Both these young men were then educated at court, but

other chiefs taken prisoner, including John Moydertach (John of Moidart), Chief of Clanranald, were held in Edinburgh Castle.

Following the death of James V, in 1542, a struggle for power developed between his widow, Mary of Guise, and Cardinal Beaton, who were strongly pro-French and the Regent, the Earl of Arran, who was under English influence. Arran envisaged renewed disturbance in the West Highlands as a means of advancing his aims, and the fact that in 1543 both Donald Dubh (the grandson of John Lord of the Isles) and John Moydertach managed to escape from Edinburgh Castle seems more than coincidence.

### Rebellions of Donald Dubh

Donald Dubh reached Islay where his people with great rejoicing proclaimed him Lord of the Isles. From there, with John Moydertach, and reputedly 1,800 men, he caused widespread devastation in the mainland of Argyll. Returning to Islay he was met by English ambassadors of Henry VIII, who offered him 2,000 crowns in return for his sworn allegiance. Given this encouragement the chiefs of the Isles rose to join him with the one notable exception of Sir James MacDonald of Dunyvaig.

In 1545 Donald raised a force in Ireland of reputedly 8,000 men. But the Earl of Lennox, supposed to join him in an invasion of Scotland, failed to appear. The Highlands chiefs, quarrelling over the division of the English money, deserted him and Donald died of a fever in Drogheda while attempting to raise reinforcements in Ireland. In a lifetime of fifty-five years he had known only six of freedom.

## PROSCRIPTION OF CLAN GREGOR

In the summer of 1563 the young Mary, Queen of Scots came to Argyll. She stayed in the old castle of Inveraray with her half-sister Lady Jean Stewart, who was married to the 5th Earl of Argyll. From Inveraray she crossed Loch Fyne to St Catherines, and then rode through Cowal to stay for two nights at Dunoon Castle where the keeper, appointed by Argyll, was a Campbell of Ardkinglas.

The years of Queen Mary's reign are known to have been exceptionally cold and the Queen's concern over the plight of the MacGregors, driven from Glenstrae by Sir Colin Campbell of Glenorchy, resulted in her trying to help them. But despite this the chief was executed, and the clan proscribed, in 1604.

*Glenstrae*
*The Landless MacGregors*

*Glenorchy MacGrigor's Song*
All alone I am seated
By the side of the highway
Watching for some coming wanderer
From Ben Cruachan the misty.
My hope if he can give me
Some news of Clan Grigor
With whom I spent last Sunday
In kinship and greeting.

*Oran Chlann-Ghriogair*
*Mi an shuidhe 'n so 'm onar,*
*Air comhnard an rathaid;*
*Dh'fheuch am faic mi fear fuadain*
*'Tigh' Cruachan a 'cheathaich.*
*'Bheir dhomb sgeul air Clann Ghriogair*
*No fios cionn a ghabh iad,*
*'S iad bu chuideachd a dhombsa*
*Didomhnuich so shaid.*

*Glenstrae*

The river beds of the Strae and the Orchy, gouged out and deepened as ice melted on the Rannoch Moor, converge on the east end of Loch Awe. MacGregors are known to have been in occupation there at least by the 11th century. Gregor of the golden bridles, who lived in the 14th century, gave his name to the clan. A later chief, Malcolm of the Castles, traditionally built the now vanished castle of Glenstrae, probably close to the foot of the Grey Mare's Tail, the waterfall on the east face of Beinn Eunaich where the farmhouse of Castles stands today.

The MacGregors without a charter held their land by the sword, until in the mid-15th century Duncan, Lord Campbell of Loch Awe, acquired the superiority of both Glenstrae and Glenorchy. He gave Glenorchy to Colin, the son of his second marriage, whose descendants became Earls of Breadalbane. The chiefs of the MacGregors of Glenstrae, on their succes-

sion, were enfeoffed by the Earls of Argyll. But inevitably they feuded with their neighbours and in 1556, when the 4th Earl sold his superiority of Glenstrae to Sir Colin Campbell of Glenorchy, they found themselves at his mercy. Consequently, in 1560, when Gregor Roy MacGregor applied to be invested in Glenstrae, Sir Colin refused his request. The MacGregors without land were driven to exist by cattle raiding. Many fled onto the Moor of Rannoch, but only the strong survived. Mary, Queen of Scots, when she came to Argyll in 1563, cried out in distress 'sen thai can not lief without rowmes and possessions', when told of the MacGregors' plight. She did her best to help them, granting them a free pardon and the royal peace. Writing to Alexander Menzies, laird of Weem in Perthshire, she asked him to allow homeless families to rent part of his land.

But Sir Colin Campbell persisted in his vengeance, and in 1570, when the Queen was a prisoner in England, he obtained a commission to take and execute Gregor Roy. The unfortunate MacGregor chief, captured after a year in hiding, was publicly beheaded at Campbell's castle of Balloch on Loch Tay.

Alasdair, the son of Gregor Roy, grew up totally illiterate but highly skilled as a warrior. In 1588, on reaching his majority, Sir Duncan Campbell, 7th of Glenorchy, refused him the lands of Glenstrae. Held responsible for the murder by some of his men of a royal forester in Glenartney, Alasdair was declared an outlaw. Later, pardoned by James VI, he was taken into his household. But he then became involved in a feud with the Colquhouns, which resulted in the Battle of Glen Fruin in 1603. Captured treacherously by the Campbells of Ardkinglas, he leaped from the boat in which he was being taken across Loch Fyne to Inveraray, and swam through freezing water to the farther shore.

Assured that he would be taken to England, to seek a pardon from the King, he surrendered to Archibald, 7th Earl of Argyll. Argyll kept to his word, in that he had him taken across the border before being re-arrested and taken to Edinburgh to stand trial. Condemned for treason, he was hanged his own height above eleven of his clansmen in recognition of his rank, on 20 January 1604.

The MacGregors were outlawed and the name proscribed. Licence was given to shoot them and rewards offered for their heads. The women were branded with red-hot irons to mark them as outcasts of society. An Act repealing the proscription was passed only in 1775.

## The Fletchers of Glenorchy

Glenorchy, one of the most beautiful glens in Argyll, runs from Loch Tulla to Loch Awe. The Fletchers (or Mac-an-Leisters), a sept of Clan Gregor and their hereditary arrow makers, who were traditionally the first people to light fire and boil water in Achallader, are known to have been here at least by the 11th century. Their castle of Achallader stood near the head of the glen.

The lordship of Glenorchy was granted to Sir Colin Campbell, by his father Duncan, Lord Campbell of Loch Awe in 1432. The first mention of a Campbell residence comes in 1567 when Archibald Campbell, natural son of Sir Colin Campbell, 6th of Glenorchy, received the tack of 'Auchalladour with the keeping of the hous theirof'. The Fletchers, who were vassals of the Campbells, refused to go, whereupon Archibald Campbell reputedly enlisted the aid of his half-brother, Sir Duncan Campbell, in forcing them to leave.

Sir Duncan Campbell, 7th of Glenorchy, 'Black Duncan of the Cowl', had been commissioned to control the Highlands by James VI. The story runs that he sent an English soldier with two horses to Achallader, with instructions to turn them loose in a cornfield near the castle. The Fletcher laird shouted to him in Gaelic, telling him to get them out, but the man ignored him, failing to understand, and Fletcher, losing his temper, fired a fatal shot. Upon the success of his strategy Sir Duncan advised Fletcher to disappear, promising to guard his interests until he could safely return. But having got rid of him he made legal claim to Achallader and gave the tack to his half-brother. So runs the legend, but in fact some of the Fletchers remained in Glenorchy as vassals of the Campbells until the mid-18th century when the senior branch of the family moved to Glendaruel in Cowal. The Campbells of Glenorchy continued to increase in power and Sir John Campbell, 11th of Glenorchy, was created Earl of Breadalbane and Holland by King Charles II in 1681.

## The Great Conspiracy

Colin, 6th Earl of Argyll, died in 1584. By the terms of his will his widow was left in principal charge of

their son Archibald (the 7th Earl) who was a minor, and also of the vast Argyll estates. He stipulated however that she was to be aided by a cohort of Campbell chiefs, together with Neil Campbell, Bishop of Argyll. A further clause insured that documents could only be legalised by Campbell of Calder, Campbell of Ardkinglas and the Bishop. This infuriated Archibald Campbell of Lochnell, who as next in line to the earldom (failing Argyll's two young sons) felt himself entitled to the seat of power. Lochnell had the backing of Sir Duncan Campbell of Glenorchy ('Black Duncan of the Cowl') who had quarrelled with Calder over the latter's support of the MacGregors he was attempting to evict from Glenstrae.

Calder and Sir James Campbell of Ardkinglas then fell out to the point where each tried, unsuccessfully, to kill the other. Ardkinglas died of natural causes in 1591, but his son, a weak-minded man, carried on the family feud. Further complications followed as Calder became involved in a dispute between the Earl of Huntly and the Earl of Moray. The rich and fertile earldom of Moray had been granted by Mary Queen of Scots to her half-brother Lord James Stuart, in defiance of Huntly's claim. The Countess of Argyll had formerly been married to Moray, and Calder, for this reason, upheld the cause of her son-in-law, the present earl.[36]

Lochnell, assured of Huntly's backing, organised a conspiracy which involved not only local men with a grievance, but the Chancellor John Lord Thirlestane and the Earl of Morton. They bound themselves to destroy not only Calder and Moray, but the young Earl of Argyll and his brother Colin. Once the last two were disposed of, the plotters swore to aid Lochnell in laying claim to his inheritance of the earldom of Argyll. Once this was achieved Lochnell would then grant Glenorchy his much vaunted Lordship of Lochow. Thus in effect these two men would hold almost complete monopoly in Argyll.

The 'Bonny Earl of Moray' was murdered in Fife by a party of Huntly's Gordons. Then it was Calder's turn to die. Ardkinglas found an assassin, a man called MacEllar who, armed with a hagbut,[37] crept up in darkness on Campbell of Feochan's house of Knepoch on the south shore of Loch Feochan near Oban.[38] Guided by a lighted window he saw Calder within. Three shots burst from the hagbut and his victim fell dead. MacEllar escaped initially thanks to MacDougall of Dunollie, one of the conspirators. Later however he was caught, tortured by the boot,[39] and confessed his own share in the crime and the involvement of Lochnell and MacDougall. The unfortunate MacEllar was executed but Lochnell and MacDougall, although for a time imprisoned, were released through 'some powerful influence' – presumably that of Thirlestane or Morton who, in the event of them being arrested, had promised to save them from death. Lochnell, nonetheless, despite consultation with witches, came to an untimely end.

In July 1594 the three Catholic Earls of Huntly, Angus and Erroll rebelled against the King and James VI commissioned Argyll (then eighteen) and the Earl of Atholl and Lord Forbes to subdue them in his name. Argyll raised an army and made Lochnell a divisional commander. Theories differ as to whether this appointment, amazing as it may seem, was made in ignorance of the man's duplicity or because it was safer to keep him under observation than to leave him at home. Whatever his reasons for giving Lochnell a command in keeping with his rank, however, Argyll nearly paid the price of death.

The Protestant army faced that of the Catholics at Glenlivet. The men were deployed to attack and Lochnell sent a message to Huntly to train his gunners on Argyll's standard, believing that his chief would be killed. Confusion of some sort resulted and the shots meant for Argyll missed their target while Lochnell himself fell dead. The chaos caused by this incident contributed to Argyll's defeat. The King however sent a stronger force, which overcame the Catholic Earls, and both Huntly and Erroll fled to seek asylum abroad.

## THE BATTLE FOR ISLAY

During Queen Mary's reign, Argyll remained comparatively peaceful. This was in part due to the good relations between the 5th Earl of Argyll and Sir James MacDonald of Dunyvaig, who married his sister Lady Agnes Campbell. But in 1565 Sir James was tragically killed while fighting to defend the family estates in Ireland. His son Angus, who succeeded him, married the sister of MacLean of Duart, but despite this he soon quarrelled with him over possession of the Rhinns of Islay (on the west coast of the island) which MacLean claimed to hold on a Crown Lease. Feuding continued between them and King James VI summoned them both to Edinburgh where they were immediately arrested. They were pardoned on paying arrears of rent due to the Crown, but Angus of Dunyvaig was made to leave two of his sons, his heir James, and a younger boy Angus Og, in surety for his obedience.

James MacDonald, a charming and gifted young man, became very popular as a courtier and was knighted by the King. In 1598 his father resigned the chiefship in his favour, but he then refused to produce the title deeds. Sir James was sent to deal with him and he found his father at the family home of Askomull, on the north shore of Campbeltown Loch. Angus refused to emerge, but his son set fire to the thatch, and having driven him out with smoke, arrested him and put him in irons in the name of the King. In 1598 Sir James defeated the MacDonalds in the Battle of Gruineart Strand, in which he was severely wounded.

### Loch Gruinart

Loch Gruinart, an estuary of the sea on the north-west coast of Islay, is now a sanctuary for the birds and animals, including otters and seals, which live on this wild stretch of coast. The sands on the shore at low tide shine silver under the sun, but in August 1598, according to tradition, they were stained with the crimson of blood. From the mouth of the loch on a clear day the island of Colonsay can be seen lying low on the north-west horizon. Beyond lies Mull, from where the fleet of the MacLeans of Duart swept down in a mission of vengeance inspired by a family feud.

### The battle of Traigh Ghruineard – 1598

Sir James MacDonald of Dunivaig was in Edinburgh when word reached him that the MacLeans were about to invade Islay. Returning to the island, he was just in time to have every man in arms before the attack began.

Traditionally Sir Lachlan MacLean of Duart came ashore at Ardnave Point with about 1,100 men. Sir James MacDonald, with a much smaller force, was apprehensive, but his standard bearer, who had the second sight, told him that he would win. The large army of the MacLeans, with the advantage of impetus, charged down the hill on the western side of the loch, towards what they took to be the main body of the

MacDonalds on the flats below. But Sir James, by deploying the greater part of his men in an outflanking movement, quickly surrounded the Macleans. A furious onslaught began. In the thick of it Sir Lachlan MacLean, a giant of a man, proved an easy target for a sniper. The marksman who killed him, said to have been called Shaw, apparently came from Jura. The defeated MacLeans fled from the field of battle on the death of their chief, bearing his lifeless corpse. Struck by an arrow, Sir James also appeared to be dying, but the skill of one of the Beatons, hereditary physicians to the MacDonalds, saved his life.

Loch Gruinart today is owned by the RSPB and it is one of the main haunts of the white-fronted barnacle geese that winter each year on Islay.

### Imprisonment of Sir James MacDonald

Sir James Macdonald negotiated a new agreement with James VI in 1599. Unfortunately, however, due to the interference of his wife's brother, Sir John Campbell of Calder, who schemed to get Islay himself, he failed to get an authorised charter before the King left for England in 1603. Negotiations over the MacDonalds' estates continued but the family then became fatally divided by the quarrel between father and son.

Old Angus MacDonald, convinced that Sir James was plotting against him, formed a bond of friendship with Campbell of Auchinbreck. Angus agreed to the arrest of his son and Auchinbreck then handed Sir James over to Archibald, 7th Earl of Argyll. In 1604 Argyll was commanded to present him before the Privy Council in Perth. Sir James was held without trial, first in the castle of Blackness and then, after he tried to escape, in Edinburgh Castle. In 1606 Argyll was granted a charter of North and South Kintyre and the Isle of Jura.

In 1608 Lord Ochiltree was appointed by the Privy Council to take overall control of the Southern Isles. He first sailed to Islay to accept the surrender of the castle of Dunyvaig, before continuing to Mull. In August Ochiltree summoned the chiefs of the Isles to attend him at Aros Castle, on the east coast of the island. He invited them on board the King's ship *The Moon* to hear a sermon by the Bishop of the Isles. Afterwards he asked them to dine. He then promptly weighed anchor and carried them off as prisoners to the Lowland town of Ayr. Eventually, however, on their sworn assurance that they would give all possible assistance to the Bishop of the Isles, appointed as head of a committee to make a survey of the people of his see, they were permitted to depart.

## THE STATUTES OF IONA

In August 1609 on Iona the chiefs attended a conference where the Bishop enacted the twenty-nine clauses of the Statutes of Iona, which attempted to civilise the Isles. Those in attendance swore to obey the King, the Government, and the Established Church. They also agreed to support the extension of the ministry, the establishment of parish schools, and the sending to the Lowlands of the eldest son of every man owning more than sixty cattle, to learn how to speak and write English.

Regulations, limiting the size of a chief's retinue and prohibiting the carrying of firearms, were aimed at reducing the fighting which constantly threatened islanders' existence. Also restrictions on the import and on the home production of alcohol were intended to control the inebriation which often resulted in violence. Inns were to be established for travellers, while beggars and vagabonds, who preyed upon the local people, were proscribed. The chiefs were confirmed in their rights to deal with criminals within their own domains, but they themselves in the following year were ordered to appear before the Council at stated intervals. Unfortunately the Bishop's intervention in the Isles was greatly resented by the Campbells, who thought it an unwarranted intrusion into the areas of their power.

In January 1612 Angus MacDonald, now very old and feeble, sold Islay to Sir John Campbell of Calder for a mere 6,000 marks. Sir James, still held in Edinburgh Castle, was horrified to hear of what his father had done. Turning in desperation to Bishop Knox, he wrote on his advice to the Privy Council offering to pay a rent of 8,000 marks annually for the Crown lands of Islay, or otherwise to be allowed enough money to go with his kinsmen to Ireland, or even to the Netherlands. But his proposals were ignored.

Angus MacDonald, in selling Islay, had however stipulated that were the money refunded he could withdraw from the deal. Subsequently, in September 1612, Sir Ranald MacDonnell of Dunluce, to whom

The Strand, Oronsay

the MacDonald estates in Antrim had descended, repaid the debt and acquired possession of Islay. Calder's ambitions were thus thwarted, but as the Irish landlord grew increasingly unpopular, his hopes were once more renewed. Meanwhile Sir James MacDonald, hearing of what was happening, became increasingly alarmed. The news that Coll Ciotach was on Islay added to his anxiety.

Coll Ciotach (left-handed Col), so called on account of his being ambidextrous, whose patrimony was the island of Colonsay, was already a legendary warrior. Sir James, foreseeing the danger of his presence amongst discontented people, sent instructions to his brother Angus Og, who deputised during his absence, to obey the orders of the Council under any circumstances whatever.

### The Seige of Dunyvaig – 1615

The Castle of Dunyvaig, which stands above Lagavullin Bay on the southern coast of Islay, surrendered to Lord Ochiltree in 1608. It had been garrisoned by Andrew Knox, Bishop of the Isles, head of a body of commissioners appointed by the Council to report on the conditions of his see. In the spring of 1614, when the castle was seized by a miscreant called Ranald Og, a natural son of Old Angus, in obedience to his brother's instructions, Angus Og sent Coll Ciotach to drive him out and to hold the castle himself. But shortly afterwards Angus received a warning, purporting to come from Argyll, that to surrender the castle to the Bishop would be the first step to losing everything. Accordingly, when Knox arrived, Angus not only refused to release the castle, but marooned him by ordering Coll Ciotach to burn his boats.

The Bishop, with only 70 men, found himself forced to agree that he would try to obtain a 19-year lease of Islay for Angus and the same of Colonsay and Oronsay for Coll Ciotach. Angus, having forced him to leave his son and his nephew as hostages, eventually allowed him to go. But the Bishop returned to the mainland to find, to his absolute horror, that plans were already in motion for a full-scale bombardment of Dunyvaig. A commission of lieutenancy, issued to Campbell of Calder at the end of October, empowered him to subdue the rebels in Islay. The fencible men of Argyll were called out and 200 veteran soldiers, with six copper cannon, were ordered to be shipped to Islay from Ireland.

The Bishop, desperate to save the hostages, appealed to Lord Dunfermline, the Lord Chancellor, who agreed to let a man called George Graham, a Gaelic speaker who knew Angus Og, go to Islay to try to arrange their prompt release. Dunfermline supplied a warrant, supposedly authentic but actually fraudulent, having not been approved by the Council. Graham, with Campbell of Danna, father-in-law of Angus Og, set off for Islay in November. Crossing by ferry from Keills to Jura, they came across two other travellers also bound for Dunyvaig. One was Campbell of Ardchattan, a relation of Calder's and the other Robert Winrahame, the Islay Herald and one of the Royal Officers at Arms, who were going, in Calder's name, to demand the surrender of the Castle.

Graham and Danna, managing to be first, found Angus and Coll Ciotach at Dunyvaig. Both were suspicious of Graham's false warrant but, as neither could read, they finally accepted it as genuine. They then released the hostages and Winrahame and Ardchattan arrived just in time to see them and their rescuers galloping headlong towards a waiting boat. Calder's ambassadors, on their own approach to the castle, were attacked and wounded by the MacDonalds, swarming like wasps from a bike, before they managed to escape.

Angus Og and Coll Ciotach, convinced of the validity of the warrant, believed themselves to be safe. But on 14 December 1614, four ships, one of them plainly a man of war, came sailing into the island. They anchored off the southern end of the Sound and soon it was known that they carried both soldiers and ordnance from Ireland. The commander, Sir Oliver Lambert, summoned the MacDonalds to surrender and was met with the reply that they had the authority of Lord Dunfermline himself to continue holding the castle.

A parley was arranged and Lambert, having looked at it, recognised the warrant as a forgery. But Angus and Coll Ciotach were not to be convinced. The bombardment began on 1 February 1615. The cannons, landed from the ships, had been trained on the castle,

and the walls, which had withstood assault through the centuries, crumbled beneath the impact of the shot. The outer defences went first and then, on the following morning, as part of the tower itself was damaged, Angus asked to make terms. He himself, loyal to his brother's instructions, remained at Dunyvaig. But as night fell Coll Ciotach, with some of his family and retainers, escaped from the sea-gate of the castle. Sentries fired, but the boat, although holed and leaking badly, reached the Oa of Islay, from where Coll and most of his followers escaped to his own Isle of Colonsay. Angus Og, made prisoner, was taken to Edinburgh in chains. He reached the city on 23 May, the same day on which his brother contrived to escape from the castle.

## SIR JAMES MACDONALD'S REBELLION – 1615

Sir James MacDonald received a message, smuggled into the prison, that Campbell of Calder had obtained a secret warrant for his execution from the King. Knowing that to stay meant death, he made a bid to escape. His breakout from Edinburgh Castle was contrived by two MacDonalds, one the son of Keppoch, the other of Clanranald. With them he managed to get to Skye and from there to sail across to Eigg. Word somehow reached Coll Ciotach, who joined him with about 150 men. Others came in and with a force 300 strong they landed first on Colonsay before reaching Islay on 23 June.

In darkness their men stole round the rocks below the fortress of Dunyvaig. Then in the first faint light they rushed the outer defences. The Constable, Alexander MacDougall, was killed, and with the gates burning and the water supply cut off, the garrison was forced to surrender. Sir James wrote from Islay to all who might possibly help him. To Bishop Knox he explained how he had only broken ward because of the news he had received 'that his Majesty, by his secret warrant, had given over my life in the Laird of Calder's hands'. But his appeal was ignored. The news that his brother Angus Og had been executed in Edinburgh drove him to take revenge.

He sailed from Islay to Kintyre with upwards of 400 men. Landing at Kilkerran (now Campbeltown) he sent runners with the fiery cross throughout the length of Kintyre. The response exceeded his expectations, as his former vassals, armed with all they could find, rallied to the call to arms. But in Edinburgh the Privy Council had summoned the Earl of Argyll, then living in England, to take command of the army. By the end of August he had set up his headquarters at Duntrune, where 400 regular soldiers, including gunners, were shipped in from Ireland.

Acting on the information that Sir James was encamped in Kintyre, near Tayinloan, Argyll divided his army, advancing himself through Knapdale, while Sir John Campbell of Calder landed a large force on the islands of Cara and Gigha to block off escape by sea. Coll Ciotach, with a fleet of about 50 small ships, was nearly trapped in west Loch Tarbert, but somehow managed to escape and made it in safety to Islay. Meanwhile Sir James MacDonald, warned by the smoke of fires lit by the MacDonalds of Largie on Cara, had time to form up his men to face the approaching enemy. But almost as the first shots were fired they fell back in confusion before the professional soldiers. The fight was quickly a rout and Sir James, forced into a boat, only just avoided capture.

Eventually he too managed to reach Islay. There on the islet of Oversay, off the point of the Rhinns, the men who had survived the battle are said to have begged to be allowed to die at his feet. But further resistance he knew could only worsen their fate, and as smoke from the hills to the east warned again of impending danger, he finally bade them farewell and sailed in deep sadness for Ireland. Sir James took refuge in the Spanish Netherlands, where, by the greatest of ironies, he met his old enemy Argyll who, ruined financially by the campaign, had been forced to leave the country. Both died eventually in England.

## The Murder of MacDuffie of Colonsay

Following the defeat of Sir James MacDonald in 1615, Coll Ciotach quickly turned his coat. Argyll wrote to Lord Binning on 13 October 1615, describing how Coll Ciotach, who had surrendered Dunyvaig and the island fort of Lochgorm before cannon had even been landed, 'has offered to do such service as may relief himself'.[40] Then again, on 25 October, he told him, 'this day Coll Ciotach has returnit to me and brocht witte him nyneten of the rebellis that followit Sir James . . . One of thame had the commandement of fourtie men, his name is MacDuffie'.

Coll Ciotach's hatred of Malcolm, chief of the MacDuffies of Colonsay, was based on his former treachery to the MacDonalds of Dunyvaig. In 1605, confused by the quarrelling between Angus MacDonald and Sir James, he had made a secret bond of friendship with Donald Campbell of Barichbeyan, promising mutual protection against anyone except 'the Erliss of Argyll and their special friends'. Somehow this had been discovered and, in 1618, when Malcolm MacDuffie was released from prison following an amnesty, Coll Ciotach exacted cruel revenge.

In February 1618 he sailed into Colonsay from Rathlin, supposedly to settle an argument over land. But hardly had his ships reached shore before the fighting began. MacDuffie, chased across Colonsay, fled at low tide across to Oronsay, past the still standing stone cross on the causeway, which marked it as a place of sanctuary. But this proved no protection. Cornered in the south of the island, he heard the noise of pursuit. In a last desperate effort he stripped to his vest and boots, plunged into freezing water and swam across a strong current to the islet of Eilean nan Ron (Seal Island). There, crouching below thick strands of seaweed hanging down from the rocks, he heard his enemies shouting as they searched for him in a boat. The splashing of oars grew fainter and he thought he had managed to escape . . . but a seagull, stooping in curiosity, betrayed him and the MacDonalds returned. Pulling him into the boat, they rowed off and put ashore on Colonsay. Dragged to a standing stone, he then was placed before it and shot, the MacDonalds removing the bullet to save for another day.

# CHAPTER 5: Civil War

My dear and only love, I pray
That little world of thee
Be governed by no other sway
Than purest monarchy;
For if confusion have a part,
Which virtuous souls abhor,
And hold a synod in thine heart,
I'll never love thee more.

As Alexander I will reign,
And I will reign alone;
My thoughts did ever more disdain
A rival on my throne.
He either fears his fate too much,
Or his deserts are small,
That dares not put it to the touch,
To win or lose it all.

And in the Empire of thine heart
Where I should solely be,
If others do pretend a part
Or dare to vie with me,
Or if Committee thou erect,
And go on such a score,
I'll laugh and sing at thy neglect,
    And never love thee more.

But if thou wilt prove faithful then,
And constant of thy word,
I'll make thee glorious by my pen,
And famous by my sword;
I'll serve thee in such noble ways
Was never heard before;
I'll crown and deck thee all with bays,
    And love thee more and more.

James Graham, Marquess of Montrose 1612–1650

*The National Covenant – 1638*

The insistence of King Charles I on the use of the English Prayer Book within the Scottish churches led to great religious controversy which divided the kingdom.

In the spring of 1638 Lord Lorne, eldest son of Argyll, went to London and told the King most bluntly that the bulk of the Scottish people would not, under any circumstances, submit to interference in the form of their worship. The King, greatly offended, then turned to the Earl of Antrim (a likeable if rather feckless young man who had inherited the Irish property of the MacDonalds of Dunyvaig), asking him to do all that he could to enlist the aid of the Catholic families in Scotland.

In the summer of 1639, Lord Lorne, on the death of his father, became the 8th Earl of Argyll. He also officially signed the National Covenant, just made compulsory for those holding office by an Act of

68

Parliament. The General Assembly of November 1638 abolished episcopacy and deposed all clergy who opposed the Covenant.

On 2 June 1640, the Scottish Parliament, known as the Estates, elected Argyll as its President. The clerical state was abolished and the signing of the Covenant became obligatory. In 1641 the King attended the parliament in Edinburgh where, having agreed to the demands of the Covenanters, he honoured many of their leaders. Argyll, with whom he had quarrelled so bitterly, was created a Marquess. (The foreword to this book was written by his direct descendant – His Grace Ian, 12th Duke of Argyll.)

In August 1643, when war had broken out in England between the King and his parliament, the Scottish Government raised an army to support the Parliamentarians. Subsequently, on 13 October, the Scottish Estates and Assembly approved the Solemn League and Covenant, which pledged the support of the Scottish Presbyterians to the English Parliamentary Party.

### Marquess of Montrose

Those who opposed it in Scotland included the young Earl of Montrose. He believed that the subjection of Royal authority would lead to anarchy, and also that, on a personal level, Charles I had been betrayed. Convinced that the King's cause in Scotland could still be saved he rode to Oxford to find him. There he was joined by Antrim, and together they at last persuaded the King to allow them to co-ordinate in raising armies in Scotland and Ulster.

Montrose, with typical honesty, was blunt about his chances. 'If it please Your Majesty to lay your commands upon us for this purpose, your affairs will at any rate be in no worse case than they are at present even if I should not succeed.' Montrose, created a Marquess by Charles I, was made Lieutenant-General of the Royal Army in Scotland, while Antrim became General of the Isles and the Highlands. It was then agreed between them that in April, Montrose would raise the men of the Borders as Antrim landed 2,000 men in Argyll. He adhered to the plan, but having taken Dumfries, was forced back across the border into England. Meanwhile nothing was heard from Ireland. But eventually news arrived that Alasdair MacColla MacDonald (son of Coll Ciotach) had been commissioned by Antrim to lead an expeditionary force to Argyll.

### Invasion of Alasdair MacColla MacDonald – July 1644

On a beautiful July day in 1644 a small fleet of three ships sailed into the northern shore of Loch Sunart below the castle of Mingary. They carried the expeditionary force sent from Ireland by the Earl of Antrim to aid the Marquess of Montrose. The commander was Alasdair MacColla MacDonald, now a man of nearly forty, renowned for his feats of arms in the recent war in Northern Ireland. The skies were apparently cloudless, but as he set foot on Scottish soil, an explosion, loud enough to be heard for miles, apparently rang through the heavens. Logically, it must have been either a clap of thunder or an earth tremor, but to the men of Alasdair's army it seemed to portend good fortune.

The castle of Mingary[41], although virtually impregnable from the sea, had an entrance on the landward side, connected by a drawbridge over a moat. Alasdair traditionally took the castle by piling burning wood against the door, until the garrison, overcome by smoke and short of water, had to make unconditional surrender.

He expected support in Ardnamurchan, but the local people, terrified of their landlord, Sir Donald Campbell of Barbreck, dared not rise in arms. More disappointment followed when messengers, sent to the Earl of Seaforth and to MacDonald of Sleat, returned with the news that neither would declare for the King. Alasdair had agreed with Antrim that on landing in Scotland, he would try to draw off the main force of the Covenanters while Montrose advanced. But news then came of the defeat of Charles I at Marston Moor. Montrose had been seen afterwards at Carlisle, but that was all anyone knew.

Alasdair, increasingly despondent, was apparently about to return to Ireland, when the capture of at least one of his vessels by ships of the English government cut off escape by sea. He then had to move quickly to avoid being cornered on the peninsula. So leaving a garrison in Mingary, he began the long march across Scotland to Blair Atholl, where, largely by good fortune, he found the Marquess of Montrose.

### Montrose's Campaign in Argyll 1644–45

In December 1644 Montrose invaded Argyll. Marching westward from Perthshire he encamped at Clifton, near Tyndrum, before sweeping down Glen Lochy into Glenorchy where the soldiers of the Irish contingent burned and pillaged on the farms. Reaching the old village of Barrachastalain[42], above Dalmally, Montrose is said to have forced the MacNabs, who were hereditary blacksmiths to the Campbells of Glenorchy, to sharpen the swords of his men. He then divided his forces to make a pincer attack on Inveraray.

Alasdair MacColla with his Irishmen went down the south shore of Loch Awe to cross over the old drove road from Durran to Loch Fyne and thus approach the town from the south, while Montrose led his main army down Glen Aray, and perhaps sent a contingent down Glen Shira to close in from the east.

A short way down Glen Aray, on the eastern side of the river, the ruins of the village of Carnish lie beneath a clump of Scots pine. Here on a dark night the houses blazed into the sky. The glow on the horizon was seen in Inveraray and the Marquess of Argyll managed to escape in a fishing boat before the Royalists fell on the town. Miraculously many people did survive as Inveraray burned. Some, reaching boats, managed to get across Loch Fyne. Others took refuge in the woods or in the shielings on the hills. How many died is not known – a figure of nearly 900 is given for the whole district – and traditionally 'not a cock crew or a chimney smoked within twenty miles of Inveraray'.

But in January, when news reached him that a large army, commanded by General Campbell of Auchinbreck, was approaching, Montrose led his army northwards, round the head of Loch Awe. Once facing west, in the Pass of Brander, the men struggled over the perilous track along the slope of Cruachan, into the full force of a gale. Suddenly, before them, a weird figure blocked their way. An old woman stood there, her white hair streaming in the wind. The men recoiled in terror, thinking her to be a witch, as Montrose shouted orders that none must touch a hair of her head. They pushed on through the Pass of Brander to reach Loch Etive where her magical powers seemed proven as the wind suddenly dropped, leaving calm water in the usually turbulent narrows of the Falls of Lora.

Montrose and his army were ferried across by Campbell of Ardchattan, whose mother was a MacDonald, on the promise that Ardchattan's own land was spared. From Benderloch Montrose led his forces through Appin and thence round Loch Leven into Lochaber. But on reaching the foot of Loch Lochy, he heard that Auchinbreck was behind him, and he then made his famous outflanking march to defeat him at Inverlochy. Further success followed but, in September 1645, Alasdair MacDonald left Montrose to make renewed invasion of Argyll. He did so with the assistance of Sir James Lamont, who although taken prisoner at the battle of Inverlochy had been released in May 1645 on the sworn promise that he would call out his men for the King.

In August, after his victory at Kilsyth, Montrose summoned him to his camp. Sir James then agreed to attack the Campbell lairds of Cowal, but he begged most earnestly for support. Alasdair MacColla's invasion of Argyll, when he supposedly deserted Montrose, may in fact have been made at his instigation. Certainly it was made with the collaboration of the Lamonts for, on reaching Rosneath, on the Gareloch, he was ferried across Loch Long into Cowal by Archibald Lamont, brother of Sir James.

Landing at Strone Point, they marched together to burn the little town of Strachur, on Loch Fyne, before laying waste to Glendaruel. The Campbells were quick to take revenge. In May 1646, a strong force commanded by Campbell of Ardkinglas came in by ship from Ayrshire to land below Toward. Nine cannons, trained on the castle, began a heavy bombardment. The unfortified east range was badly holed and people within it killed.

Sir James Lamont then agreed to surrender both Toward and his fortress of Ascog, near Loch Fyne, on honourable terms. Men from both garrisons were held in Toward until taken by boat to a court martial, held within the kirk of Dunoon. On Sunday 14 June, they were executed, actually within the churchyard, by enemies insensible with fury. Over a hundred were shot or dirked[43], while their leaders, cadets of Clan Lamont and their tenants, 36 in all, were first hanged from a tree and then cut down and buried alive. Later, when the tree was cut down, the roots were said to spout blood.

Sir James Lamont and his brother Archibald, taken to Inveraray, survived imprisonment in irons. But his wife and five little children, three of whom died of starvation, were left to live off whatever they could find on the shore. Sir James Lamont's estates were restored to him in 1661, but he never again lived at Toward Castle, which gradually became a ruin.[44]

*Devastation of Argyll by Alasdair MacColla*
*MacDonald 1645–47*

In June 1646, following the surrender of Charles I to the government, Alasdair, then classed as a rebel, continued to lay waste to Argyll. The devastation that he caused, in what became a personal vendetta against the Campbells, is vouched for by family histories.[45]

In 1646 Alasdair laid siege to Craignish Castle[46]. The laird, Archibald Campbell, 'the most daring strong man of his time', who could clear the now vanished moat in a single leap, defied him. He is said to have held the castle for three weeks with only 250 men against Alasdair with a force 1,500 strong. According to legend Alasdair finally withdrew when, having imbibed too heavily at a banquet, he wandered within range of the castle and was wounded by an arrow.

Most people in Argyll, terrorised by the continual attacks of marauding parties of raiders, took refuge within castles 'even as foxes when hunted hard doo to their holes'. Family histories of Argyllshire families record many tales of grim happenings. The Campbells of Kilberry, sending out a flagon of ale, deceived him into thinking that their castle was so well provisioned that he did not attempt a siege. Others were not so fortunate. The Campbells of Melfort, having buried everything valuable, left a feast upon the table at Melfort House. His men having consumed it, one of them set the house on fire, but was hanged by Alasdair for doing so.

Quick to take offence, Alasdair, insulted because Baron MacCorquodale of Phantisland (on the north shore of Loch Awe near Kilchrenan) failed to lower his flag in salute, destroyed his castle on an island in Loch Tromlee. Seldom did he show mercy, but in the hamlet of Barrachander, above Loch Tromlee, an old woman ran out of her cottage to tackle one of his men who was about to set fire to her roof. Alasdair, seeing this happen, ordered him to leave her alone, shouting in Gaelic that such a brave old woman did not deserve to die.

A few resistance leaders emerged. One was little John Campbell of Bragleenbeg near Loch Scammadale on the west coast of Lorn. The River Euchar runs from Loch Scammadale and Alasdair, joined by the MacDougalls and the MacAulays of Ardencaple, marched up the glen. The families of the townships took refuge in a barn at a place called Lagganmore.

Alasdair ordered it to be set on fire and only little John Campbell, with one woman, escaped through the blazing thatch. Little John, once captured, was given a choice of how to die. Asking to be put inside a circle of his enemies, he threw his sword in the air. Instinctively they all glanced upwards and he ducked between them and escaped.

Another who defied him was Zachary MacCallum of Poltalloch of whom Alasdair is reported to have said that 'only lime, stone and MacCallum are friends of Argyll'. Alasdair approached Duntrune across the Crinan Moss. But a man from Dunadd ran ahead to give warning and, on reaching the castle, he was met by well-aimed fire. He was riding a mare called Nic Laomain (Miss Lamont). She must have been a present from the Lamonts and, saying 'hot are these spits round nic Laomain's feet', he got quickly out of range. He then forced the mare to swim into the River Add, where turning her head into the current, she almost drowned him. But thanks to his enormous strength, he managed to pull her round and make her swim over to Knapdale. There he encamped, but the MacCallums pursued until, probably in the valley of the Add, they met in a fierce encounter. Alasdair, his sword broken in hand-to-hand fighting, saw Zachary MacCallum close in.

Alasdair, almost defenceless, knew he must die. But one of his men, seeing what was happening, threw another sword over a dyke and Alasdair seized it, then killed Zachary, his greatest antagonist in Argyll.

*The Mill of Gocam-Go*

Following his defeat of Zachary MacCallum, Alasdair seems to have moved from Glassary into the Eurach Gorge, the glen to the south-west of Loch Awe. Before the last Ice Age the loch drained down through the gorge before reaching the sea. Part of the water course now comprises Loch Ederline and the little Loch Ceann a Choin (Loch of the Dog's Head). A short way past this second loch, a side road branches off the main road to lead to Kilmichael Glassary. About half a mile above Loch Ceann a Choin a knoll below the road would seem to be the site of the water mill of Gocam-Go.

Two ancient Scots pines stand above a piece of levelled ground (at the foot of the knoll) above the burn called the Allt Bealaich Ruaidh (River of the Red Pass) where the mill most probably stood.

Many years before, during his childhood in Colonsay, his nurse, by dropping a piece of blue wool in a cauldron, had told fortunes at Halloween. Predicting Alasdair's future, she had promised that all would go well with him until he reached a place called Gocamgo. According to local legend he had burned many townships without finding one of that name, but now as he raised his standard, the flag wrapped itself round the pole, contrary to the wind, and a coin sprang from the ground just as she had foretold.

Alasdair, discovering the name of the place, is said to have wept like a child, and for a short time, to have lost all control.

Clearly the local people, emboldened by rumours that a government army approached, were now retaliating. It is said that scythes were straightened as weapons and the retreating invaders pelted with stones and divots.

Another legend tells how Alasdair, marching down Kilmichael Glen, was fired on by men from a small fort on the island in Loch Leathan. The man beside him was killed and he spurred his horse forward out of range.

## Defeat of Alasdair MacColla – 1647

In May 1647, as the army commanded by General David Leslie marched westwards from Edinburgh, the Royalists, under Alasdair, retreated to Kintyre. There, because of his negligence in failing to defend Tarbert, he was surprised on the west coast near the Point of Rhunahaorine.

Alasdair believed he was safe. Always superstitious, he had resorted to divining the whereabouts of his enemy from the age-old method of studying the lines on the shoulder bone of an ox. The sage he consulted saw soldiers crossing a bridge. Relieved, he took this to be the one spanning the Leven at Balloch, quite forgetting that a bridge had just been built over the Douglas, just a few miles south of Inveraray.

Alasdair is said to have been at Old Largie, home of the MacDonalds of Largie, when a breathless runner came in with the news of Leslie's advance down Kintyre. His cavalry had already reached Tarbert, only some 20 miles away. Alasdair's badly equipped, and apparently disheartened force, was overcome in a battle at Rhunahaorine, as the old castle was called, by Leslie's well trained troopers the next day.[47] Seeing his position hopeless, Alasdair fled on his faithful

mare Nic Laomain who jumped a near impassable chasm in a burn near Rhunahaorine before reaching the shore. There he found an old patched boat but it could not hold his gallant mare. So drawing his sword he ran it through her heart rather than leave her to the enemy. Once afloat his followers clung to the gunwale. Unable to take them aboard, he cut off their fingers to stop the unseaworthy boat from being swamped. Known to have reached Gigha, Alasdair then escaped to Ireland, where, having joined the Catholic army to fight against the Protestants, commanded by the Earl of Inchiquin, he was killed in the following November.

His father, Coll Ciotach, who reached Islay, was besieged by a contingent of General Leslie's men at Dunyvaig. Coll Ciotach, on recognising the Captain of Dunstaffnage (an old acquaintance who had formerly been his jailer) amongst them, came out and demanded a bottle of whisky before returning to the castle. Eventually made a prisoner, he was taken to Dunstaffnage Castle on Loch Etive. It was either then, or during his former term of imprisonment at Dunstaffnage, that Coll Ciotach was roped in to help with the harvest, having a strong pair of arms. Word that Dunstaffnage was being too lenient with his prisoner somehow reached Inveraray Castle, whereupon the Marquess immediately sent a party of horsemen to see what was going on. Fortunately for Dunstaffnage, a man of his own called MacKellar, a very fast runner, happened to overhear what was said. Escaping from the castle, he outran the horsemen across the ridge that separates Loch Awe from Loch Fyne, known as the Lechan Muir.

Reaching Portsonachan, he crossed Loch Awe by the ferry, leaving his pursuers on the shore. But once on the road through Glen Nant they rapidly overtook him, galloping on the faster ground. He just managed to get within sight and earshot of Dunstaffnage and to shout out 'Coll Ciotach is in irons' before they caught up with him. Figures, too distant to recognise, understood the message so that, on reaching the castle, the riders found the prisoner they had been sent to look for, safely shackled to the dungeon wall.

Despite his friendship with Dunstaffnage, Coll Ciotach, tried and convicted of treason, was hanged above a cleft in the rocks near the castle from the mast of his own ship. Reputedly he is buried below the second of the chapel steps, a last request granted by the Captain of Dunstaffnage, so that in the next world 'they could share a pinch of snuff'! From Rhunahaorine many of the islanders got away by sea, the fact of their boats being in readiness suggesting that Alasdair, when attacked, was actually on the point of embarkation. But those left on the mainland, including many MacDougalls, had no alternative other than to retreat down the peninsula to the supposedly secure fortress of Dunaverty.

The massacre of Dunaverty was one of the most tragic events in the whole history of Argyll. General Leslie reached the castle on 31 May, but MacDonald of Sanda, who had taken command, refused to surrender on the promise of quarter. Leslie then attacked, and by taking an outer ditch, cut off the castle's water supply, apparently led in by a pipe. The garrison within the fortress, reputedly 500 strong, surrendered to the King's mercy as death from thirst became inevitable. It is said that they were left to the clemency of men whose friends and relatives had been burned alive in the barn at Lagganmore.

Sir James Turner, Leslie's Lieutenant General, describes how on 'coming out of the castle (they) were put to the sword, everie mother's sonne, eccept for ane young man MacCoull (MacDougall) whose life I begged to be sent to France.'[48] Bishop Guthrie, another eyewitness, blamed much of the slaughter on the army chaplain, John Nevoy, who, describing the curses that fell upon Saul for sparing the Amalekites, encouraged indiscriminate butchery. It is said that even David Leslie, finding himself walking over the ankles in gore, turned in disgust to Nevoy saying, 'Now, Mr John, have you not once gotten your fill of blood?'

The bodies, according to local tradition, were thrown over the cliff, and skeletons found in the sand during the 19th century, after a particularly high tide, are believed to have been those of the victims.

### Glencairn's Rising 1653

King Charles I was executed on 30 January 1649. Upon the news reaching Scotland his son, Charles, was proclaimed king. In May 1650 the new king sailed from Holland to land at the mouth of the Spey. His coronation took place at Scone on 1 January 1651 when he received the crown from the Marquess of Argyll.

Charles II was defeated at Worcester in 1651. Commonwealth rule was then established in Scotland.

General Monck became Cromwell's lieutenant and the Marquess of Argyll, believing that he was acting in the best interests of his country, reached an agreement with the Protector. In March 1653 the Earl of Glencairn took command of the Royalist forces in Scotland and Argyll's sons, Lord Lorne and Lord Neil Campbell, joined him to the great sorrow of their father. In 1655 Lord Lorne was pardoned. But two years later, on refusing to take an oath of allegiance to the Commonwealth, he was imprisoned and held in Edinburgh Castle.

## RESTORATION OF CHARLES II
## 1660 TRIAL AND EXECUTION OF
## THE MARQUESS OF ARGYLL 1661

Following the restoration of Charles II in 1660, Lord Lorne was well received by the King. His father the Marquess of Argyll, refusing to believe that the new king hated him, determined to go to court. The dogs howled round the castle of Rosneath, where Argyll was then living. Local people, knowing this to be a bad omen, beseeched him not to leave. Ignoring their pleas he set out for London. Arrested at Whitehall, he was held prisoner in the Tower for five months. He was then taken to Edinburgh by ship, where he was made to stand trial. Convicted on the evidence of letters that he had acted against the Royalists, he was sentenced to death. He died with great courage, swearing upon the scaffold that he had not conspired towards the death of Charles I.

### Acquisition of Lands of MacLean of Duart by Archibald, 9th Earl of Argyll 1674

The 9th Earl of Argyll was restored to his father's earldom (although not to the marquisate) in 1663. The enormous cost of the Civil War impoverished many Scottish families. Sir Allan MacLean of Duart was reduced to bankruptcy and in 1674 the 9th Earl of Argyll, having bought up his debts, took possession of his estates. Argyll garrisoned Duart Castle to enforce his authority, but in the following year the MacLeans refused to pay the dues owed to him as their superior. The case was taken before the Privy Council, who gave verdict in favour of Argyll. Thus the lands of the MacLeans of Duart in Mull became his territory.

Carnasserie Castle, near Kilmartin

## Carnasserie Castle

Carnasserie Castle, on a hilltop at the head of Kilmartin Glen, was placed to overlook the entrance to the pass which runs eastward to Loch Awe. Known locally as 'The Bishop's Castle', it was built between 1565–72, apparently on an earlier foundation, by John Carswell, a noted Gaelic scholar, who was rector of Kilmartin. Following the Reformation, Carswell was made super-intendent of Argyll, before becoming Bishop of the Isles. His castle consists of a tower house of five storeys, connected to a hall house of lower height. A narrow stair from the ground floor leads up to the solar, or private sitting room, adjoining the Great Hall.

The Bishop was closely connected with the 5th Earl of Argyll and his wife (the half-sister of Mary Queen of Scots). An armorial panel over the doorway, on the north side, carries the Gaelic inscription 'Dia Le Ua Nduibh(n)e' – 'God be with O Duibhne (Argyll)'. The Bishop died in February 1572 on a day of a terrible storm. Long afterwards was it remembered how his coffin had been taken by boat to Loch Etive for burial at Ardchattan Priory. The boatmen, strug-gling against gigantic waves, had been so weary that they had pulled into the bay at Muckairn, on the south side of the loch, for food and one or two drams. Still the wind had raged and the boat, unsurely moored,

had drifted away to end up eventually on the opposite shore at a place known to this day as the 'Bishop's Point'. Fortunately, from there, it was but a short way to the Priory where the Bishop was at last laid to rest.

In 1594 John Campbell of Ardkinglas, accused of complicity in the murder of Campbell of Cawdor some two years before, was imprisoned in the castle. Threatened with torture, he nonetheless became friendly with his jailer, Donald Campbell, to the point where 'efter meikle drinking of wyne', which Ardkinglas had brought from his cellar, Donald allowed him to escape.

Carnasserie remained with the Carswells until, in 1643, it was granted by the superior, the Marquess of Argyll, to Dugald Campbell of Achnabreck. The initials S.D.C.–L.H.L. above an entrance on the west side stand for Sir Dugald Campbell of Achnabreck and his wife, Lady Henrietta Lindsay. During the time of the Civil War, when the area round Kilmartin was raided (c1646) by the men of Alasdair MacDonald's following, Carnasserie itself apparently escaped attack. But forty years later, following the execution of the 9th Earl of Argyll, the MacLeans of Mull seized the opportunity to revenge themselves on his followers for the loss of the chief's land of Duart. Sailing to the mainland, they set fire to Carnasserie and laid waste to everything within the surrounding district.

Achnabreck claimed, in 1690, that it had been besieged by a force including Lachlan MacLean of Torloisk and other leading MacLeans, together with his own neighbour Archibald MacLachlan of Creaganterve. That following its surrender they 'did barbarously murder Alexander Campbell of Strondour, the petitioner's uncle,' wounded about twenty of the garrison, drove away 60 horses, and 'did set fire to the said house of Carnasserie and burn it to ashes'. He claimed £20,000 Scots in compensation for its destruction, but no attempt was made to repair the shell.[49]

Sir Dugald's wife, the former Lady Henrietta Lindsay, returned to the castle, where, amidst the charred remnants of the house, she found the family charter chest, thrown aside by the invaders, but still miraculously intact. The castle was afterwards repaired. The oven beside the huge fireplace in the kitchen, and the stoup through which water could be poured from outside into a barrel, are probably innovations of this time.

Carnasserie, although now roofless, is one of the best examples of a 16th-century castle in Argyll. Entrusted by the Malcolms of Poltalloch to the then Office of Works in 1932, it is now maintained by Historic Scotland.

## MONMOUTH'S REBELLION 1685

In 1681, the Catholic Duke of York, acting as his brother's commissioner in Scotland, was persuaded by Royalists, who included the MacLeans of Duart, that he was threatened by Argyll's increasing power. Accordingly, in July 1681, the government introduced the Test Act to ensure that the Duke of York's succession would not be endangered by his religion. All those in authority, within both Church and State, were compelled to acknowledge the Confession of Faith of 1560, and to promise to uphold the existing forms of civil and ecclesiastical government.

Argyll was not a Covenanter, but he swore to the Test Act only 'in so far as it was consistent with itself', words construed as treachery. Held in Edinburgh Castle on a charge of high treason, he was tried and sentenced to death. But on the eve of his execution, his step-daughter, Lady Sophia Lindsay, came to say farewell. A page carried her train and Argyll, who was a small man, changed clothes with him and escaped from the castle undetected.

Argyll managed to reach Holland, and in 1685, following the death of Charles II, he collaborated with the Duke of Monmouth in an attempt to overthrow James VII and II. Sailing from Holland he first landed in Islay before continuing to Kintyre. From there he marched to Tarbert, where his ships and land forces congregated on 27 May. He wanted to try to take Inveraray, but was persuaded to head for the Lowlands where the majority of the people supported the Covenanters' cause. Encamped at Duntreath Castle in Stirlingshire, he enlisted a local man to guide him over the Kilpatrick hills. But in a night march the guide lost his way. His army scattered, Argyll himself was taken prisoner while trying to ford the River Clyde. Taken in chains to Edinburgh he was condemned to death without trial. Many of his followers were executed, or else sent as convicts to plantations in America.

### Depredation of Argyll 1685–91

At home their land was ravaged, both by the army of occupation from Perthshire, and by local people who, in the absence of authority, renewed old family feuds. An inventory, headed 'Depredations of Argyll 1685–91' and drawn up after the restoration of the 10th Earl, catalogues the thefts. Everything was taken, from cattle to the minister's wigs.

Argyll's eldest son, Archibald, Lord Lorne (who became the 10th Earl) made a spectacular escape from Inveraray. Hiding in Glen Shira, he was saved from starvation by a farmer called Munro who, while feeding his cattle, threw a packet of oatmeal from beneath his plaid, over the rock behind which he knew Lorne was crouching. Mixing the meal with water in his shoe, Lorne, starving as he was, afterwards declared it to have been the best meal he had ever had. Pursued by soldiers, who had discovered him, he jumped the River Shira, where it narrows between rocks, at a place still called 'Argyll's Leap'. From the head of Glen Shira, following the old track to Loch Awe, he reached what was then the island of Inistrynich. From there, he somehow reached Holland where the family had a small estate.

Returning to Scotland after the Revolution of 1689, which resulted in the overthrow of James VII and II, he was created Duke of Argyll by William III, in 1701, in honour of his loyalty to the Presbyterian cause.

*The Treaty of Achallader 1691*

The now ruined tower house of Achallader stands beside a whitewashed farmhouse some half-mile to the north-east of the head of Loch Tulla, three miles north of Bridge of Orchy. The castle was built *c*1600 by Sir Duncan Campbell, 7th of Glenorchy, on the site of the earlier castle of the Fletchers, to defend the northern part of his territory. His descendant Sir John Campbell, 12th of Glenorchy, was created Earl of Breadalbane and Holland by King Charles II in 1681. Although originally a Jacobite, he transferred his allegiance to William and Mary following the defeat of the Jacobite army at Dunkeld in 1689. A devious character, he was nonetheless a true Highlander who knew that the problems of his people were based largely on poverty. Appointed by the Privy Council to deal with the disaffected chiefs, he summoned them to meet him at Achallader in June 1691. The castle had been burned by Jacobite soldiers in 1689 but a tented camp was built. Some, like MacLean of Duart, travelled from afar. But old MacIain of Glencoe, a magnificent figure well over six feet tall, white haired and erect for all of his 80 years, had only a few miles to come.

Cameron of Lochiel, as spokesman for the chiefs, asked first for compensation. He insisted that £20,000 was needed to pay off debts incurred in the recent war, and to allow the purchase of superiorities from overlords. Also he asked for full indemnity, the right to carry arms, and the assurance that nothing more than an oath of allegiance was required. Finally, the now exiled James VII and II must authorise the Jacobites' submission and the officers be allowed to stay in Scotland or go to France. Breadalbane, having made provisional agreement to these requests, then promised that £12,000, the limit the government would provide, would be paid to the chiefs, in ratio to their rank. With this they had to be satisfied and the Treaty of Achallader was signed, on 30 June 1691, by Major-General Buchan and Sir George Barclay for the Jacobites, and by Breadalbane for the Government.

King William sanctioned the agreement, and the money reached Scotland in September. Breadalbane made distribution from his castles of Kilchurn on Loch Awe and Balloch at the foot of Loch Tay. Reporting to the Master of Stair, Secretary of State for Scotland, he famously declared, 'The money is spent, the Highlands are at peace and there's no accounting between friends.'

Finally, on 21 December, Major Duncan Menzies, an envoy sent to James VII and II, arrived exhausted in Edinburgh with the King's discharge to the clans. Consequently the Highland chiefs, albeit with reluctance, did sign the oath of allegiance before the deadline, 31 December 1691, with the one notable exception of old MacIain of Glencoe.

## THE MASSACRE OF GLENCOE

Glencoe descends from the Moor of Rannoch through a steep ravine until it reaches the wider strath below. It is a place where, even on a fine day, a sinister atmos-

Buachaille Etive Beag, at the head of Glen Coe

The Massacre of Glencoe memorial

phere seems to linger, perhaps because of the closeness of surrounding massive hills. The two great mountains, Buachaille Etive Mor and Buachaille Etive Beag, the Shepherds of Etive, surmount the head of the glen. To the north the sheer wall of the Aonach Eagach forms an effective barrier, while to the south the range of mountains, which include Bidean nam Bian (3,766 ft), the highest mountain in Argyll, appear at first sight to be impregnable. But some steep passes do run through these seemingly inaccessible heights. In particular the rough track through Glean Allt na Muidhe, to the head of Glen Creran in Appin, although deeply covered in snow, proved to be a way of escape in February 1692.

In 1689 the MacDonalds of Glencoe supported the Jacobite cause at Killiecrankie under Viscount Dundee. Much has been made of the fact that on their way home from Killiecrankie, taking the shortest way through Glenlyon, they raided the lands of the Campbells of Glenlyon. They took almost everything, from animals down to the cooking pots, making destitution inevitable during the coming winter months. But despite this act of brutality, the action taken against them was not, as has sometimes been suggested, merely an act of revenge.

The chiefs of the Highland clans were ordered to swear allegiance to King William before 1 January 1692. Most complied, but old MacIain of Glencoe, perhaps through stubbornness and pride, left it until the last moment. On reaching Fort William, in the last week of December, he found that the Governor of the garrison, Colonel Hill, did not have the authority to accept his oath. The old man therefore had to struggle on through snowdrifts to Inveraray where he finally did sign the declaration on 6 January 1692.

But he was six days late and the Secretary of State, the Master of Stair, saw this as a reason to exterminate 'that sept of thieves', as he called the MacDonalds of Glencoe. The orders came down the military line. Colonel Hill, on receiving them at Fort William, detached a company of regular troops from Argyll's Regiment and sent them, under the command of Campbell of Glenlyon, to Glencoe. Most of the soldiers were Highlanders, although the Non-Commissioned officers were Lowlanders, posted in to stiffen the regiment when formed. Six of the Highland men were actually MacDonalds, but acting under orders they had no option but to obey when, in the dark of a February night, the word came to attack.

Old MacIain, according to tradition, was living in his farm in Gleann Allt na Muidhe, and not in his house of Invercoe farther down the glen. Awakened by the sound of hammering on the door, he opened it and was shot at point-blank range. Mortally wounded he fell into the arms of his wife who, cruelly assaulted by the soldiers, died herself the next day. Thirty-eight people in all were massacred in that February dawn. Orders had been given to block the passes, but thanks to what may have been deliberate negligence, many managed to escape.

Amongst other stories is that of Ronald, who was warned of some unseen calamity by a priest with the second sight. Throwing his plaid over the head of soldiers, who were dragging him out of his house to be shot, he carried his wife Helen up the hillside as his staghound leapt at the throats of the men trying to pursue them through the snow. Hiding in a secret hollow above Alld-na-féith – the Quagmire Burn – on the side of Ben Chrùlaiste, they saw a man, obviously exhausted, struggling through the blizzard carrying a child. He proved to be a soldier named Dorset, now like themselves a fugitive. He had rescued the child of the widow with whom he had been quartered at risk of his own life. He told them that Colonel Hamilton, with a company of 400 men, was on his way to block the passes at the head of Glencoe to prevent any escapes. Struggling on together, they reached Helen's father's house, in Glenfruin in Appin, from where they continued to Barnstaple where the English Dorset's family took them in. Here, soon after their arrival, Helen and Ronald's son was born.

The story reveals humanity, whatever the truth of the tale. But the name of the glen is still synonymous with tragedy after over 400 years. Nonetheless the real significance of what happened lies in the ensuing outcry. The public conscience was awakened. An enquiry was urgently demanded, and an event which a few years before would have gone virtually unnoticed was now of national importance.

## THE RISING OF 1715

Archibald, 1st Duke of Argyll, and his son John who succeeded him, remained loyal to the crown. John, 1st Earl of Breadalbane, however was adept at changing sides. Although originally a Jacobite he swore allegiance to William III. But in 1715, when the Jacobites rose in arms to try to restore the Chevalier, son of James VII and II, to the throne, he reverted to his former adherence. Too old himself to take to the field he sent Colin Campbell of Glendaruel to represent him. On Glendaruel's suggestion a force of about 4,000 men advanced upon Inveraray in the hopes that the Duke of Argyll, 'Red John of the Battles', in command of the Government Army, would be lured from his headquarters in Stirling to defend his own country.

The plan failed. Argyll refused to be drawn and his brother, Archibald Earl of Islay (later the 3rd Duke) called out the County Militia and brought arms and ammunition to Glasgow. General Gordon, the Jacobite commander, a soldier who had made his name in Russia, did make a demonstration against Inveraray, which proved to be the last attack on the town. From their camp at the foot of Glen Shira, the men of Gordon's army had a clear view down Loch Fyne. The company of MacGregors was commanded by Gregor Ghlun Dubh (Gregor of the Black Knee) of Glengyle, one of his officers being none other than his uncle, the legendary Rob Roy.

The sight of a heavily laden ship, beating up the loch against the wind, proved temptation too strong to resist. Rob Roy is said to have led some of his men round the head of the loch, to a point where the ship neared the shore. Wading out, with muskets held above their heads to keep the powder dry, they boarded her and took the crew prisoner in the name of King James. Their triumph was short lived. Without siege weapons Gordon could not take Inveraray Castle. Then, at the sound of shouts and firing, after a Highland soldier gave a password in Gaelic to a Lowland man in the defence, which made him think that a relief force had arrived, he gave the order to retire. The MacGregors, much to their fury, had to abandon their prize. Their anger was obvious, yet soon it was being whispered that Rob Roy was in collusion with 'Red John of the Battles', as the Duke of Argyll was known.

Following this incident a detachment of Breadalbane's men confronted the Argyllshire Militia at the head of Lochnell in Lorn. The soldiers, preparing to fight, threw off their plaids, but their leaders, reluctant to shed Campbell blood, agreed that the Breadalbane men could march off safely after laying down their arms. Both sides cheered heartily, and Islay, arriving at this moment, had to concur with the agreement.

John, Duke of Argyll, commanded the Government army at the battle of Sheriffmuir, while Breadalbane's men fought for the Jacobites. But following the end of the hostilities most of the Jacobites were offered indemnity upon the surrender of their arms.

## ROB ROY MACGREGOR IN ARGYLL

An unfortunate and perhaps unforeseen result of the amnesty was that the Highland farmers were left without means of defence against the cattle raiders, who 'lifted' their beasts usually at night. Campbell of Achallader, factor to Breadalbane, warned that when the nights turned longer and the cattle stronger it would be worse, 'for a dozen armed men may rob and plunder the whole side of the country . . . the garrison of regular troops are in no way fit to curb them.' Rob Roy MacGregor, himself once a dealer, saw the chance to make money by organised protection. Those paying him 'blackmail' could sleep more easily at night.

The MacGregors as a clan were still proscribed, but the Earl of Breadalbane allowed Rob Roy to rent the farm of Brackley, in Lorn, in 1714. The farm of Brackley (Breac-leathad, meaning the speckled slope) rises to the south-east above Dalmally. Coming from that direction, an old track leads to the ruined village of Auchtermally, where the people who lived there in Rob's day made horn spoons. Farther up the hill was Barran, now marked by a single shepherd's house, but then a farming township.

Famously, Rob Roy was returning from the market, then held at the foot of Glen Strae, when from one of the thatched cottages came a delicious smell of stew. Bending low to enter the door, he asked the good wife to give him some, but she told him brusquely, in Gaelic, to be gone. Unabashed he borrowed a bucket, conveniently beside the door, which he filled with water from the burn. Returning to the cottage he threw water over the fire above which simmered the stew pot. The room filled with blinding smoke. When it cleared Rob Roy had vanished. So too had the stew!

Farther up the track, on the saddle of the ridge above Glen Shira, was the Tailor's Village, where people from both directions came to have their homespun cloth made into clothes. In Glen Shira itself, the Duke of Argyll, 'Red John of the Battles', gave sanctuary to Rob Roy and allowed him to build a house there in 1717. Rob Roy with the help of six of his ghillies put up the then conventional living room and byre, separated by a wattled partition. The walls, much ruined, stand beside the River Shira. Just above is a deep hollow, a natural 'beef tub' into which cattle could be driven and held.

Rob, who was popular in Inveraray, remained

The remains of Rob Roy's house in Glen Shira

on good terms with his landlord. His sporran, together with a letter warning the Duke of a would-be assassin, are on view in Inveraray Castle.

It would seem to have been while he was living in Glen Shira that Rob Roy attended a funeral. The man who died was one of the MacCorquodales of Phantisland, who sometime after the destruction of their castle on the island in Loch Tromlee, on the north side of Loch Awe, by Alasdair MacColla MacDonald, had moved to the old town of Inveraray. However, although no longer on Lochaweside, they kept their right to be buried in the Pre-Reformation church of Kilchrenan where the funeral was due to take place. The mourners gathered in the house of the deceased in Inveraray. Men came from far and wide. But then it was remembered that it was unlucky to leave for a funeral until the first cock had crowed. It was winter time and during the long night much hospitality was dispensed. Drams flowed freely, so that by the time of the first light of dawn, most were in a merry mood.

They departed up Glen Aray, stopping at intervals to refresh themselves with some of the local uisge beatha brewed in hidden stills. Portsonachan was reached eventually, on the south side of Loch Awe, from where a ferry conveyed them to Taychreggan on the opposite shore from where they walked, some rather unsteadily, up to the ancient church. The funeral took place with due solemnity before the wake in the local inn. There someone unfortunately claimed that the MacCorquodales, having left Phantisland, had forfeited their rights of burial in Kilchrenan. At this pandemonium broke loose. Men flew at each other with their cromachs (shepherd's crooks), Rob Roy laying about him with gusto. The dogs who had followed their masters now joined in the fight. The furniture in the inn was smashed to pieces and it was only with great difficulty that the MacCorquodales and their adherents were pushed on to the ferry to return. This, it is said, was the last time one of that family was ever buried in Kilchrenan.

## THE RISING OF 1745

A state of emergency began in August 1745 when a horseman, who had ridden hard from Dunstaffnage and crossed Loch Awe by Portsonachan Ferry, galloped into the town. He came with a letter from Donald Campbell of Airds, the Duke's factor in Morvern, containing a message, passed on from the Minister of Ardnamurchan, that Prince Charles had landed in Moidart. The Sheriff, Campbell of Stonefield, sent it on immediately to Lord Milton, the Justice Clerk, who he knew to be at the Duke's castle of Rosneath. The Duke (Archibald 3rd Duke of Argyll) was in fact there himself, together with his cousin Jack Campbell, colonel of the Earl of Loudoun's new Regiment of Foot.

The memorial at Culloden, Invernessshire

Colonel Campbell's men saw action in the first week of November when Gregor MacGregor of Glengyle, a nephew of Rob Roy, led a band of his men into Cowal. Colonel Campbell, with his three companies, then promptly crossed Loch Fyne and quickly overcame and dispelled them. A summons to arms proved disappointing, for few appeared to enlist, but the Duke, as Lord Lieutenant of the County, called out the Militia. Meanwhile within the old castle of Inveraray great activity began as arms, stored since the last emergency of 1715, were brought out to be cleaned.

On 29 November, 500 broadswords and the same number of muskets with ammunition, ordered from Liverpool, were landed by Government ships. But the broadswords came without belts, then urgently demanded from the Provost of Glasgow, who must have known where they could be found.

Colonel Jack Campbell had written to his father, Major-General Campbell, to describe events. The General, having recently fought at Fontenoy, was with his regiment near Brussels. But knowing that there was not a single high-ranking officer in Scotland under the age of 70, he immediately asked to be released. He landed at Inveraray on 21 December, just as it was known that the Jacobite Army, retreating from England, was heading north back to Scotland. He promptly sent 50 men to hold the Pass of Tyndrum, and promised reinforcements for Stirling. But on word of the Jacobites nearing Glasgow, the troops remained at Dumbarton.

Nearly all the principal landowners of Argyll had by now obeyed the call to arms. The men led by the lairds, and in some cases the ministers, converged upon the cross at Inveraray. By 5 January 1746, 1,198 men had arrived and most were encamped around the town. The weather was cold and wet and many of the Duke's trees, as well as wood stored for the new castle, of which the foundations were laid, ended up on camp fires. The General himself became depressed, writing that 'Inveraray is a very pretty place but there's so great difficulty of access to it, so many ferries and when heavy rains come, which are very frequent, there's no having any intelligence.' To add to the discomfort there was then a shortage of food. By the end of January only 14 days' supply of oatmeal remained in the camp. The situation seemed desperate until word was received of two food ships sailing north from Liverpool.

## Culloden and After

You understand it? How they returned
    from Culloden
over the soggy moors aslant, each cap at the low
    ebb no full tide could pardon:
how they stood silent at the end of the rope
unwound from battle: and so to the envelope
of a bedded room came home, polite and sudden.

And how, much later, bards from Tiree and Mull
would write of exile in the hard town
where mills belched English, anger of new school:
how they remembered where the sad and brown
landscapes were dear and distant as the crown
that fuddled Charles might study in his ale.

There was a sleep, long fences leaned across
    the vacant croft. The silly cows were heard
mooing their sorrow and their Gaelic loss.
The pleasing thrush would branch upon a sword,
a mind withdrew against its dreamed hoard
as whelks withdraw or crabs their delicate claws.
And nothing to be heard but songs indeed
while wandering Charles would on his olives feed
and from his Minch of sherries mumble laws.

*Iain Crichton Smith*

## The end of the Rising 1746

The battle of Culloden, on 16 April 1746, when the
Argyll Militia fought with distinction, finally defeated
the Jacobites. The Duke of Cumberland, commander
of the Government Army, then ordered a diligent
search for the Prince's supporters throughout the
Highlands and the Isles. The Duke of Argyll protested
about the cruelty shown to some of his own tenants
in Morvern and his cousin Major-General Campbell,
in command of the Government Army in the north
of Scotland and the Isles, did all in his power to
restrain the harshness of his officers against people
powerless to resist.

Following the Prince's escape from the field,
General Campbell conducted a search for him throughout the Western Isles. In Skye, Flora MacDonald was
arrested for her part in taking the Prince from Benbecula

across the Minch. General Campbell, having issued
orders that she was to be treated with special care,
took her upon his own warship, the *Furnace*. On
reaching the Sound of Kerrera, he despatched a letter
to Neil Campbell, the Captain of Dunstaffnage, asking
him and his lady to entertain 'a very pretty young
rebel' for several days. General Campbell returned to
Inveraray on 18 August, where, on word of Charles
having reached France, he stood down the Militia.

## THE APPIN MURDER

The persecution of Jacobites, after the Rising of 1745,
led to the murder in Appin of the government factor,
Colin Campbell of Glenure, and to the trial and
execution of an innocent man. James Stewart of
Aucharn, or James Stewart of the Glens, as he was
known, died convicted of an assassination, of which
he was almost certainly innocent, and his sentence
has since been recognised as a notorious miscarriage
of justice. The 'Appin Murder', so well, if fictionally,
described by Robert Louis Stevenson in *Kidnapped*,
resulted from the cruelty shown to the local people
after the Jacobite Rising of 1745 by those invested
with authority.

The estates of the men who had risen for Prince
Charles were forfeited and Colin Campbell of Glenure
in Appin, known locally as 'The Red Fox', became

The site of the Appin Murder

Crown Factor of the lands of Charles Stewart of Ardsheal and the Camerons of Lochiel. Glenure evicted tenants suspected of Jacobite sympathies including James Stewart of Aucharn, who as he rightly guessed, was sending money to his half-brother Ardsheal, now an exile in France.

On 14 May 1752 Glenure rode from Lochiel and headed south for Appin. Reaching the north shore of the narrows of Loch Leven he crossed by the ferry. The ferryman, Archibald MacInnes, a man with the second sight, begged him not to continue down Loch Leven but to go home through Gleann Fhiudhaich. But Glenure in fact was heading for Ardsheal, where he intended to carry out evictions. Ignoring the ferry-man's warning, he continued along the bridle path across the Leitir Móir. Suddenly a shot rang out and Glenure, struck by two bullets in his side, fell from his horse a dying man. Two men, never identified, were seen running away from the scene. One is thought to have been Allan Breck Stewart, as described in Stevenson's book.

A cairn, erected in 1970, on the site of his murder, stands in a forestry plantation some two miles to the west of Ballachulish Bridge (NN 032593). The identity of the assassin, although known to at least one local family, has never been publicly exposed. As it was, James Stewart of Aucharn, known as Séumas a'Ghlinne (James of the Glen), a farmer in Appin, arrested on purely circumstantial evidence, was taken to Inveraray to stand trial. The court was presided over by no less a person than the Lord Chief Justice, Archibald 3rd Duke of Argyll. Much has been made of the fact that 11 of the jury of 15 men were Campbells, but as jurists in those days had to be landowners it was difficult to find others in Argyll of a different name. The Government were terrified of another insurrection. It was only six years since Culloden. Appin was known to be harbouring rebellious Jacobites. An example had to be made.

James Stewart of Aucharn became the scapegoat. Found guilty of being 'art and part to the crime', he was condemned to death, sentenced to be hanged. The execution was carried out at Ballachulish, the body being left on the gibbet in proof of the penalty for disobedience. A monument which stands on a knoll called Cnap a'Chaolais, above the south end of Ballachulish Bridge, was erected by the Stewart Society in 1911 to commemorate James Stewart, who was executed there on 8 November 1752.

Shortly before his death, Stewart famously stated, 'If I am innocent grass will not grow on my grave', a prophesy proved to be true. He was buried in Keil Chapel, which stands, now largely ruined, in a quiet place above the sea. While surrounding stones are much overgrown, the one beneath which he lies remains bare.

The real name of the murderer remains a mystery to this day. Some 20 years later the young laird of Ardchattan was in Paris where, at an inn, he met a plainly impoverished Highlander, claiming to be Allan Breck Stewart, who swore that he was innocent of this famously unsolved crime.

*Inverawe*

A laird's house in the 18th century, Inverawe House was the scene of one of the most famous ghost stories

The memorial to James of the Glen

of Argyll. Duncan Campbell of Inverawe was at home when a fugitive rushed in and touched hearth, making the old claim of sanctuary. Breathless, he panted out that he had killed a man and was being hunted for his murder. Duncan hid him in a niche behind the panelling in a room at the top of the house. Hardly had he done so when pursuers arrived to tell him that the man he was sheltering had killed his own foster brother. True to his word he did not betray him but that night as he lay sleepless the ghost of his foster brother appeared. Pulling back his cloak to reveal the terrible stab wounds that had killed him, he commanded: 'Shield not my murderer.'

Duncan refused to obey but the next night the ghost appeared again whispering the same words. Unable to bear the presence of the assassin in his house, he took him to a cave on Ben Cruachan. Returning to Inverawe he believed himself rid of the ghost. But that night the murdered man appeared again and this time he uttered the prophetic words: 'Farewell; we shall meet again at Ticonderoga.' Duncan, who had never heard of the place, had no idea what he meant. As a soldier with the rank of Major, he went out to Canada from where he sent back barrels of seeds and young trees to be planted at Inverawe. Then, when taking part in the siege of the French-held Fort Carillon, he was told that the Indian name for it was Ticonderoga. Some say he saw the ghost again, but all that is known for certain is that, convinced that he was doomed, he died in the ensuing battle in 1758.[50]

The existing house of Inverawe, altered and extended in the Scottish baronial style during Victorian times, was subsequently remodelled by Sir Robert Lorimer in 1913–14 and by L.C. Norton in 1953–4 when it was reduced in size.[51] Currently owned by Robert Campbell-Preston, it is now the headquarters of the universally known Inverawe Smokehouse, established by Robert and his wife Rosie in 1980.

## Castle Stalker

Castle Stalker, or more correctly Castle Stalcair, the castle of the Hunter, on its tiny island in Loch Laich, is a famous landmark of Appin. This district of Lorn, held by the MacDougalls from the 12th century, passed through marriage to the Stewarts of Innermeath c1386. Following the murder of Sir John Stewart, Lord of Lorn, in the family chapel of Dunstaffnage (see p. 22) his legitimised son Dugald was granted Appin.

By slaying the assassin Allan MacCoull, a kinsman of the MacDougall chief, Dugald Stewart apparently avenged his father's death. A granite stone, on a crag in the Episcopal Church of Portnacroish, bears the following words:

> 1468. Above this spot was fought the
> bloody Battle of Stalc, in which many
> hundreds fell, when the Stewarts and the
> MacLarens, their allies, in defence of
> Dugald, chief of Appin, son of Sir John
> Stewart, Lord of Lorn and Innermeath,
> defeated the combined forces of the
> MacDougalls and the MacFarlanes.

The castle is believed to have been built by Alan Stewart of Appin in the mid-16th century although, according to another source, it was granted to him by James V, who died in 1542. With its distinctive crow-stepped gables, Castel Stalker is a tower house of four storeys, each of a single room. An outside stair leads to the first floor containing the great hall.

The lands of Appin appear to have been sold by Duncan Stewart of Appin to Sir Donald Campbell of Ardnamurchan and Airds in 1620. According to a well-known tradition the Stewarts then lost the castle when the young chief Duncan exchanged it during a drinking bout for a birlinn (an eight-oared galley) with Donald Campbell of Ardnamurchan. The New Statistical Account of 1845 states that the building was 'new roofed and floored' by Sir Donald Campbell of Ardnamurchan in 1631.

In 1686, following the execution of the 9th Earl of Argyll, the Stewarts regained the castle for a brief four years. But forfeited as Jacobites in 1690, they were forced to surrender it to the Crown. In 1745, when word of Prince Charles Edward's landing in Moidart reached Inveraray, Castle Stalker was garrisoned by the 3rd Duke of Argyll. In March 1746 Captain Caroline Scott, a man notorious for his cruelty, came there to order the collection of all axes from the people of Airds and the island of Lismore. Following the defeat of the Jacobites, he laid waste to their lands and destroyed all that they owned within the surrounding district. The castle, by then roofless, was sold by the Campbells in the mid-19th century. Repurchased by Stewarts in 1908, it then changed hands again, in 1966, to another family of the same name, who have since restored it as a home.

## Ardsheal

The promontory of Ardsheal, on the south shore of Loch Linnhe, is today one of the most beautiful and peaceful places in Argyll. The present house stands on the site of the earlier building, home of the Stewarts of Ardsheal, which was burned to the ground by Government soldiers in 1746.

Charles Stewart of Ardsheal, a man of enormous stature and famed as an expert swordsman, commanded the Appin Regiment of the Jacobite Army. Returning from the disaster of Culloden he was forced to take to the hills where he found shelter in caves. General Campbell ordered the sequestration of his cattle, but concerned for the young family, he had the milk cows returned. He wrote to Isabel Stewart, Ardsheal's wife: 'Madam, your misfortune and the unhappy situation Ardsheal has brought you and your innocent children into . . . makes my heart ache. I have taken the freedom of ordering two bolls of meal, out of my own stores, to be left here (at Airds) for which I desire you to accept for yourself and the little ones.'

Thus the Jacobite family survived. But three months later, when the General had left Appin, the infamous Captain Scott returned. Lady Ardsheal fled to the shelter of a barn where, as her house burned to the ground, her daughter Anne was born. Nothing on the place was spared, even the fruit trees cut down. Eventually, after many narrow escapes, Ardsheal reached France. There his brave wife joined him and they never returned to Argyll.

Duncan, the second son of Charles and Isabel Stewart, went to America. He became a Revenue Officer in Boston and married Anne Erving, daughter of the Governor of the town, with whom he eventually returned to Scotland. In 1769 his elder brother and his cousin Dugald, chief of the Stewarts of Appin, both died and Duncan succeeded as 6th of Ardsheal and 10th of Appin. Ardsheal was restored to him in 1784 and the original part of the present house, built on the site of the burned-out ruin, is attributed to him.

Duncan's grandson, who was a bachelor, sold the estate in 1844. It changed hands again when bought by Mr Alexander Cameron in 1906. He left it to his daughter Bridget, who became Mrs Sutherland. Ardsheal House was sold to pay death duties in 1968, but was bought back by Neil, youngest of the Sutherland's twin sons, in 1994.

From the *Song of Breadalbane*
Duncan Ban MacIntyre 1722–1812

O hail to Breadalbane!
Where deer, roes, and fawns are found,
There, lying so lightly
In long hollows of rushes and grass,
The stags and the hinds are around me,
Lying on the shoulder of every bush,
They are sharp-eyed and sharp-eared,
Watching what may come round them at night.

*O failt air Braid-Albann;*
*Gheibhteadh feidh ann is earban is minn;*
*'S iad 'n an luidhe gu guanach*
*Ann am feadanan luachrach isi clob,*
*Na daimh 's na h-eildean mu'n cuairt dailbh*
*'S iad an luidhe air guala gach tuim,-*
*'S iad gu bior-shuileach, cluasach,*
*'Feitheamh clod thig mu'n cuirt duibh 's an an oidheh*

# CHAPTER 6: The 18th Century to the Present Day: *'when sheep could safely graze . . .'*

## AFTER THE '45

The suppression of the Jacobite Rising of 1745 proved a landmark in the history of Scotland and in particular in the Highlands and the Isles. In 1746 the government, by abolishing hereditary jurisdiction, reduced the power of the chiefs whose strength had hitherto lain in the number of men they could summon to arms. Subsequently the great castles, built primarily for protection and as armouries for weapons, were in many cases abandoned for more comfortable homes. New houses were built for elegance of design.

Relieved as they were of their authority, the landlords, at least in most cases, were forced to live off their estates. 'Improvement' became the order of the day. Inevitably the reverse side of the picture resulted from an increase in rents. The tacksmen who had held land from their chiefs mainly on a military basis were amongst the first to leave. Countless families who went, mostly to America, in the later part of the 18th century, gave their reason for doing so as impoverishment due to high rents. Later many others were to follow as small farms were amalgamated into larger units to make way for flocks of sheep.

The First Statistical Account, 1791–99, contains many examples of how the scenery was changed. Although during the last decades of the 20th century, the hills were covered with swathes of coniferous trees, so nearly 200 years ago almost the reverse occurred. The great influx of sheep into Argyll resulted in many people seeking work within the towns. The Second Statistical Account of 1845 gives details of the numbers of men employed in the fishing industry and in the many distilleries by then existing on the mainland and Isles. It was in fact the developments of those times which set the scene in Argyll as we know it today.

## AGRICULTURAL IMPROVEMENTS AND CHANGES IN USE OF LAND

The hills and glens of Argyll still carry traces of the agricultural improvements of the 18th and 19th centuries. Stone drains can be discovered, often in working order, and dykes built to surround enclosures largely date from that time. The grass is still greener round the ruins of circular lime kilns, where limestone was burned until it split enough to be crushed and spread on the ground.

Ploughing became widespread as 'Small's Plough', pulled by two horses, replaced the old Anglian plough which needed at least four animals to haul it through the ground. All farms in Argyll grew Scotch bear, a form of barley excellent for brewing ale, but white oats, which give a higher yield than grey, were then becoming popular. Most farms grew a patch of flax, which, like the wool from the few sheep which were kept, was spun and woven at home.

Most significant of all are the patches of ridge and furrow where potatoes were grown. Potatoes were the staple food of most Highland families by the end of the 18th century and the now deserted patches, often covered in heather and bracken of the 'lazy beds', remain as a sad reminder of the grim struggle for existence faced by many Highland people of that time.

The improved land carried more stock. Better hay was grown and the introduction of turnips in around 1720 meant that cattle, which before had been killed in November for lack of fodder, could now be kept through the winter. Cattle had been the mainstay of the Highlands since before recorded time. It was not long since a man's wealth had been reckoned on the number of beasts that he owned. Formerly when the animals were killed in the winter the meat was salted and kept in tubs, but in the latter part of the century, as demand for Highland beef grew, they became more valuable on the hoof. Great droves of cattle were herded down to the markets of Crieff, Falkirk and elsewhere, and the trade boomed during the wars with Europe when the government needed salted meat to feed the army and the navy.

In 1762 some farmers from Annandale first rented land in Argyll. Previous to this the hills had been grazed only in summer when people drove their animals to the *airidhs*, or upland grazings, to keep them away from the crops. The old Scottish sheep, which were small and white-faced, needed to be housed in winter, but now it was found that the black-faced sheep, introduced from the Borders, a bigger animal with a long thick fleece, was capable of standing all weathers. Their numbers increased rapidly, altering the appearance of the country. The Reverend Joseph MacIntyre, minister of the united parishes of Glenorchy and Inishail in Lorn, and contributor to the First Statistical Account, wrote that 'the hills and muirs which some years ago were covered with heath and course herbage are, since the introduction of large sheep into the country, gradually getting a richer sward and greener hue.'

Others of his calling were more honest, describing the poverty of people who, thanks to the influx of sheep, were now trying to make a living on small patches of ground or by seasonal fishing and any other work that could be found. The worst affected were those living on the coast and on the islands. Sadly the local people, with their small boats, could not compete with the larger, better equipped vessels, sponsored by the Fisheries Society. Also the kelp industry – the burning of seaweed to make fertiliser – almost ended following the Napoleonic wars, when it became cheaper to import barilla, and to make chemical manures.

The situation became more desperate when the potato blight, *phytophthora infestans*, devastated the crops of potatoes from 1839 onwards for several consecutive years. The government did take action. Sir Edward Coffin, appointed by the Treasury to enquire into the need for assistance, arranged for the distribution of food and seed corn from depot ships lodged in the main firths. But the problem of supporting so many people on so little available land remained insuperable and many were forced to leave. The lamentations of those who went are voiced by Duncan Ban MacIntyre, the poet of Glenorchy. Duncan, who was born in 1722 in Glen Fuar, a place too remote for a school, grew up totally illiterate. But another wrote down his verses and through them we hear his heart cry against the falling of the great Scots pines and the coming of the sheep which drove people from the land.

The old road to Dalmally crosses the hill below the monument, erected to Duncan's memory in 1860. William and Dorothy Wordsworth, who came this way in 1803, were told that the crofts of Stronmilchan, which they saw below in Glenorchy, had been laid out by Lord Breadalbane for soldiers returning from the European Wars, perhaps to prevent discontent and emigration.

On departing, local people left a footprint, cut in the turf below the monument, before heading downhill for Inveraray for the ship on which they would embark. Now below the hilltop lies a forest once more. The wheel has gone full turn.

*The Military Roads*

A great programme of road building in the Highlands began in the 1720s when the government commissioned General Wade to supervise the scheme of construction. It was continued after peace was restored in 1746 and by 1757, only eleven years later, £130,000 had been spent on this project. Among six new roads constructed was the one from Dumbarton to Inverary, which joined near Tyndrum with the highway from Stirling to Fort William. Landlords were compelled to send some men – the number reckoned by the size of their estates – for a limited period to help with the work. Most of it was done however by the red-coated soldiers who sweated and toiled in the mud, often in freezing wet weather, with only picks and shovels to do most of the exhausting work. The new roads encouraged travellers who nonetheless had to cross most lochs and rivers by ferry. Dorothy Wordsworth describes how her unfortunate horse was terrified out of its wits by the boatmen yelling at it in Gaelic as they crossed the ferry over the Falls of Lora at the narrows of Loch Etive, now spanned by Connel Bridge.

Transport by boat in fact continued to be the main form of travel in many parts of the north-west of Scotland until the great increase and improvement of roads following the First World War.

## The Felling of the Trees

Prior to 1745, trees were so little valued that the great Scots pines of the Old Caledonian Forest in Glenorchy were bought by some Irish adventurers for as little as a plaque apiece (about two-thirds of the old penny). Then as the forests in northern England ran out, iron-masters looking for charcoal began to buy timber in Argyll. Dorothy Wordsworth describes the blackened stumps of the trees felled in upper Glenorchy, and as she drove through the Pass of Brander her eye was caught by a beautiful sailing ship which had deposited bags of charcoal for the furnace at Bonawe.

The business had been established in 1753, some 50 years before, when a group of ironmasters from the Lake District, headed by Richard Ford, had built the ironworks on the shores of Loch Etive. The furnace, ore shed and charcoal sheds, now in the care of Historic Scotland, give an idea of the industry that once existed here. A pier was specially constructed so that ships could unload iron ore conveniently nearby. Two years later a second foundry was built by the Duddon Company of Cumbria at Furnace on the west shore of Loch Fyne on land leased from the Argyll estate. Archibald, 3rd Duke of Argyll, sold many of the woods on South Lochaweside to the Company in 1754. Charcoal burned in the now-ruined kilns on the hillside was carried in panniers by strings of ponies, walking head to tail, across the drove roads to Loch Fyne.

## The Slate Quarries of Easdale and Ballachulish

During the 18th and 19th centuries the newer and better houses were roofed with slates rather than thatch. Slates were quarried in several places, but the biggest workings were on the island of Easdale, some nine miles south of Oban, and at Ballachulish on the northern border of Argyll. The quantity of slates cut at Easdale and on the adjoining smaller island of Ellanbeich resulted in the latter becoming joined to Seil by a causeway of quarry waste.

During the first part of the 18th century the business was expanded as slates were shipped out on vessels

The old road at Rest and Be Thankful

trading between the ports on the Clyde and the east coast of Scotland. By 1795 five million slates were being sold annually at 25 shillings per thousand and 300 men, paid 9d to 10p a day, were fully employed. By 1869 this figure had increased to a yearly production of nine million slates, but in 1881 the main quarry at Ellanbeich was flooded during a disastrous storm and quarrying thereafter continued on a reduced scale until the time of the First World War.

The Ballachulish slate quarries were first opened by Mr Smith of Ballachulish c1693. A hundred years later over 300 men were employed and by the end of the 19th century this work force had doubled and an estimated 26 million slates were being sold every year. Output decreased steadily thereafter and the last quarry was sold in 1955. The quarries have since been landscaped and the ferries, which plied across the narrows of Loch Leven, have been made redundant by a road bridge, built in 1975. The well-known landmark at Bonawe Quarry, on the north side of Loch Etive, opened in the mid-nineteenth century and owned by J&A Gardner for over a century since 1892, currently belongs to Breedon Aggregates. The Foster Yeoman Company's granite quarry at Glensanda, on the north shore of Loch Linnhe, went into operation in 1986. Production has now reached six million tonnes a year. Eighty per cent of Glensanda granite is exported to Europe, in the company's four ships, but it has also supplied aggregate for the Thames Barrier, the M25 motorway and segments for the English side of the Channel Tunnel.

## The Fishing Industry

Fishing, from the time of the first settlers, has been a mainstay for the people of a land intersected by water and largely surrounded by the sea. During the late 18th century, as the population grew, the need for new means of employment was recognised. John, 5th Duke of Argyll, was among the more enlightened and the British Society for extending the Fisheries, founded in 1786, was launched partly at his instigation. The initiators of this scheme were prepared to put up the then very considerable sum of £7,000.

John Knox, a philanthropist who had made his fortune as a bookseller (although unrelated to the Presbyterian reformer), was commissioned by the Society to discover the potential of the fishing industry. He toured the West Highlands and in the introduction to his report he deplored the poverty of the people, particularly in the north-west of Scotland and the Isles. Optimistically however, he envisaged a new prosperity resulting from the establishment of the Fisheries Society, which would bring an end to the destitution which he so vividly described.

Knox strongly advocated the building of fishing villages, each a complete entity in itself, with a church, a school, and most importantly a pier. He was also influential in the building of the Caledonian Canal, linking Fort William to Inverness, and the Crinan Canal, stretching across Knapdale from Loch Fyne to the Sound of Jura.

## The Crinan Canal

The Crinan Canal connects Loch Fyne to the Sound of Jura, thus saving a hundred miles of dangerous sailing round the Mull of Kintyre. It was commissioned by the Trustees of the Forfeited Estates (former land of the Jacobites) to give fishermen from the north-west access to Campbeltown and to the Glasgow markets.

The work of constructing a waterway from Ardrishaig to Crinan, begun in 1793, was surveyed by James Watt and constructed by the great engineer John Rennie. Eventually it was paid for with government and private money. The canal was finally opened in 1801, and in August 1847 Queen Victoria and the Prince Consort with their children went through it while visiting Argyll. Arriving at Ardrishaig, they found a most magnificently decorated barge, drawn by three horses, waiting to pull them to Crinan. The passage through 11 locks took nearly three hours and almost the entire population turned out to cheer and wave until, on reaching the harbour, they boarded the Royal yacht.

During the following year of 1848, the canal was taken over by the Government, but the increasing size of most steamships then gradually reduced its use. Today it is busy, mainly in the summer, with yachts, motor cruisers and the smaller fishing boats avoiding the long voyage round the Mull of Kintyre.

## The Puffers

In 1893, William Hay, a farmer who used a barge to move manure about his farm beside the Forth and Clyde Canal, decided it would be more profitable to be a barge master who owned a farm. He subsequently built the Briton(length 65'8", beam 18', draft 8'4" with a 17HP engine) which proved to be the model of the little steamers called "Puffers" which, immortalised by the Inveraray-born writer Neil Munro in his stories of Para Handy, are now classics of the television screen. The puffers plied up and down the coast and to and from the islands, carrying every conceivable variety of goods.

## The Development of Steamship Services

In 1825 the first steam-driven ferry, sailing from West Loch Tarbert to Islay, provided a connection with the Clyde steamer services to the East Loch. Regular services soon went also to Campbeltown and Inveraray, where the pier was extended in 1836 at the cost of £12,000 – half of this supplied by the Fishery Board and the rest by the Duke of Argyll and the Burgh. By

1843 no less than three steamers sailed daily from Glasgow to Ardrishaig, from where fresh herrings were shipped to the Glasgow market. Passengers could then proceed through the Crinan Canal to board another steamer at Crinan which would take them to Tobermory on Mull and from thence through the Caledonian Canal to Inverness.

## The Lighthouses

To safeguard the ever-increasing amount of shipping a chain of lighthouses was built on the western seaboard of Scotland. In 1786 the creation of the Board of the Commissioners of the Northern Lighthouses – its jurisdiction extending to the entire coast of Scotland and the Isle of Man – was enacted by Parliament.

The original Mull of Kintyre Lighthouse was begun in 1786. There being no roads through the Mull, the light room and the reflecting appratus, brought from Edinburgh, were carried on men's shoulders over the hills. In Islay a lighthouse was built at Port Charlotte and another at Port Ellen by Mr W. F. Campbell of Islay in memory of his wife. The Skerryvore lighthouse, off Tiree, built by Mr Alan Stevenson, a civil engineer and uncle of Robert Louis Stevenson, was under construction in 1843.

## The Growth of Distilleries

An increase in distilling and brewing did bring prosperity to some places, particularly to Kintyre and Islay, and later to elsewhere. The art of making whisky, first known as uisge beatha (aquavitae), the spirit of which Coll Ciotach was so excessively fond, is believed to have come from Ireland as early as the 15th century. Originally flavoured with thyme, mint, aniseed, and other herbs, it gradually changed form until Thomas Pennant, visiting Kintyre in 1722, referred to the whisky then being distilled there as 'modern liquor'. In 1797 the government was faced with a crisis as the cost of financing the war in Europe drained the Exchequer, and consequently the licence on all excisable liquors was drastically increased. Many distilleries were ruined, those in Campbeltown going out of business for at least 20 years.

Illegal distilleries however became increasingly profitable. Whisky was made all over Argyll, usually in stills beside burns in remote places in the hills. In Islay, in 1795, the Excise Officer found about 90 stills,

Puffers at Crinan

some holding as much as 80 gallons. The trade was most highly organised to the point where Excisemen, riding round the country, needed bodyguards armed with pistols to protect them. By 1820 it was estimated that at least half of the whisky made in Scotland came from illicit stills. Much of the rent was paid in whisky and in parts of Argyll the majority of labourers and cottagers supported large families on the profits from their stills. Alfred Barnard, in his book on distilleries, says that 'up to the year 1821 smuggling was lucrative in Islay, and large families were supported in this way. In those days every smuggler could clear ten shillings a day and keep a horse and a cow.'

It is hardly surprising that the illicit distillers, when taken before the local courts, were frequently given only small fines, or in some cases even exonerated, by judges who were sympathetic landowners. In 1823 however the laws of distilling were revised, and an annual license fee of £10, together with a small duty on spirits, restored the legal industry. At least 27 licensed distillers became established in Campbeltown between 1823–27 and in Islay the total production of 12 distilleries had reached 170,000 gallons annually by 1833, a figure which had increased to 1,250,000 gallons by the mid 1880s.

Although the distilleries are now reduced in number the making and blending of whisky is still a significant industry in Argyll.

# CHAPTER 7: The Towns of the 18th and 19th Centuries and Their Importance Today

*The New Town of Inveraray*

The 3rd Duke of Argyll, who built Inveraray Castle, planned and began the New Town on the headland, known as the Gallows Foreland, which juts out into Loch Fyne. The beautiful facade, which faces east, centres round the Town House, designed by John Adam originally as the Court House and built in 1755. The courtroom was on the first floor, with the prison immediately below. Adams then designed the Chamberlain's house and Ivy House to flank it on either side. Later the Avenue Screen, linking these buildings to the Great Inn, and the arch over the road to the north, were designed by Robert Mylne.

The Great Inn, planned by John Adam, was built primarily to hold the circuit judges and others attending the twice-yearly courts. Doctor Johnson and James Boswell found it extremely comfortable, but Robert Burns, given an attic room, scratched on a window pane the famous lines which end:

There's naethin' here but Heilan pride
And Heilan scab and hunger
If Providence has sent me here
T'was surely in his anger.

The Parish Church, on the highest point of the town, planned by Robert Mylne, was completed in 1802. It is in fact a double church, the south half now the church hall. Lord Cockburn, the circuit judge, attended a Presbyterian service in English as the Gaelic one took place on the other side of the wall.

The court house, on the seaward side of the Church Square, was built between 1816 and 1820 on plans adapted by James Gillespie Graham from an earlier design of Robert Reid. The building, together with the old and the new jails behind it, has now been converted, most realistically, with the use of wax figures, to depict its use in the past.

During the 1950s, when much repair was needed, the town was transferred by the Trustees of the Argyll Estates to the joint ownership of the Town Council and the Ministry of Works. A programme of extensive restoration, financed by the Scottish Development Department, was supervised by the architect Ian G. Lindsay. As a result, Inveraray, described here only in outline, remains an almost unique example of a mid-18th-century Scottish town.

Most famous of those connected with Inveraray is Neil Munro. Born there in 1863, he left Inveraray School at thirteen and worked in the office of the Sheriff Clerk of Argyll. Leaving town to work in Glasgow, he wrote that he felt he was leaving 'everything he loved behind him' as the steamer drew away from the pier. In Glasgow his career as a journalist ended with him becoming the editor of the *Evening News*. In the meantime he had begun writing novels based on the Highlands which he loved, *John Splendid*, *Doom Castle* (about Dunderave Castle on Loch Fyne) and *The New Road* being among them. However, perhaps he is best known today for his stories of Para Handy, captain of the puffer called the *Vital Spark*, of which two television series have been made. A monument to Neil stands at the head of Glen Aray, where, lower down the glen, he spent much of his childhood with his grandmother at Ladyfield Farm.

OPPOSITE: Inveraray Main Street

Hs name is kept alive by the Neil Munro Society, founded by enthusiasts for his work in 1996.

Among other organisations the Inveraray and District Pipe Band, founded in 2005 by Stuart Liddell, is one of the most successful in recent history having won all five of the Scottish, British, European, World and Cowal Championships in 2009. In addition the Accordion and Fiddle Club and the Senior Citizens Club meet regularly throughout the winter months.

## Inveraray Castle

Inveraray Castle, in its beautiful situation at the mouth of Glen Aray, was the inspiration of Archibald, 3rd Duke of Argyll (1743–61). The original sketch, by the famous 18th-century architect Vanburgh, came to nothing but the idea was the basis for the castle we know today. The Duke was already over 60 when he embarked on his great reconstruction, both of the old castle and the old town. His achievement is all the more remarkable in view of the isolation of Inveraray in the first part of the 18th century.

'Inveraray is . . . a charming pretty place,' complained Major-General Campbell (later the 4th Duke) when in command of the Government Highland army in the Jacobite Rising of 1745. 'But there's so great difficulty of access to it, so many ferries, and when heavy rains come, which are very frequent, ther's no having any intelligence.' Roads, with a hard surface, were non-existent in the area until, in 1749, the military road from Dumbarton finally reached the town.

The castle was designed by William Morris, but the building was executed by William Adam of Maryburgh, leading Scottish architect of his day, who was appointed Clerk of Works in 1746, the year in which the foundation stone was laid. Both Morris and Adam died before the project was completed but Adam's sons, John and Robert, continued their father's work.

The framework of the castle was finished in 1758 but it fell to the 5th Duke, (Colonel Jack Campbell of the Rising of 1745) who succeeded in 1770, to complete the interior of the house. He first altered the layout of the main floor to its present form before commissioning Robert Mylne to carry out the decoration. Mylne employed two Frenchmen, named Guinand and Girard, to paint the drawing room and the dining room, which remain the finest examples of the neo-classical style in Scotland. The conical roofs on the turrets and the high roof with its gabled dormers were added by the 8th Duke in 1877–78.

The castle has twice been badly damaged by fire, first in 1875 and then on Guy Fawkes Night in November 1975. Treasures were saved by local people, who rushed to help when they saw the flames. Afterwards Ian, 12th Duke of Argyll, and his wife Iona, accomplished a great work of restoration. The Duchess herself cleaned and mended many of the tapestries. The painting and the restoration of the original paintwork, again most skilfully done, is this time the work of Robert Stewart of Inveraray, who again worked on the ceilings when they were strengthened in 2010.

Torquhil, 13th Duke of Argyll, who succeeded his father in 2001, and his wife Eleanor, have spent two years refurbishing the castle, bringing it into the 21st century with the latest in technology and wiring. Central heating, fuelled by woodchip from trees on the estate, has been installed in the private part of the castle. New bathrooms have been added, damp problems dealt with, redecoration done and an attic converted to include a playroom so that the noise made by their three children and their friends is not heard by visitors to the open part of the castle.

They have also opened the formal part of the gardens, where sweeping lawns, surrounded by rhododendrons and azaleas, are interspersed with swathes of daffodils in the spring. Both the castle and the garden are open from 1 April to 31 October. Duchess Eleanor runs the tearoom with, she insists, the best ingredients in Argyll, while Duchess Iona continues to organise the castle shop.

A famous legend tells how when Montroses's Irish soldiers invaded the old castle of Inveraray in December 1644, they murdered the Marquess's little

Inveraray Castle

Irish harpist, calling him a traitor to his country. Afterwards he was heard playing, first in the old castle, then, once it was built, in the present one, when the head of the Argyll family was about to die. He was last heard, prior to the death of Duke Neil, in 1946.

## Oban

Oban owes its early development largely to the fishing industry. Today very little white fish is landed and it is best known for its thriving shellfish catches which are exported to Europe every week. The town began with a trading station, established by a Renfrew company early in the 18th century. Later, in 1761, a custom house was built. Now called the Manor House, it is one of Oban's premier hotels.

The major expansion of the town came with the introduction of steamships carrying freight. The monument on the island of Kerrera, the island across Oban Bay, commemorates David Hutchison, inaugurator of much sea trade. This, combined with the Victorians' craze to visit the islands, and Iona in particular, in addition to the coming of the Oban and Callander Railway, brought hordes of well-off Victorians to 'do' the Hebrides. Their need to have comfortable accommodation in which to stay created a plethora of new hotels, today usually occupied by coach parties.

Herring boats sailed to the north-west and returned to unload their catches. Also the fact that the sale of salt, essential as a preservative, but at that time heavily taxed, was restricted to Government depots, provided another reason for fishermen putting in to Oban.

The town as we know it today owes much of its development to two brothers, John and Hugh Stevenson, after whom Stevenson Street is named. Said to have arrived penniless in the early 18th century, they built both a distillery and a shipyard and amassed considerable property.

More famous entrepreneurs were the McCaig family. John Stuart McCaig created one of the first employment schemes by paying stone masons to cut blocks of granite during the winter months for what is correctly known as McCaig's Tower, which gives Oban an iconic symbol of an impression of the Coliseum in Rome. The now famous landmark, which surmounts the town like a diadem, was begun in 1895 for the threefold purpose of creating a memorial to his family, of giving work to local people, and of

making a feature of interest to embellish his home town. Sadly he died in 1902 and the building remains uncompleted.

Oban distillery is the second oldest in Scotland, dating from 1794. As the town has developed it has become a service centre for administration, banks and lawyers. There is almost no manufacturing: only a small enterprise producing wetsuits. It has, however, become one of the most popular places from which to scuba dive, due to the clarity of the water, and the number of wrecks to explore.

A waterfront development on the South Pier contains shops and a restaurant, while on the North Pier there are two restaurants. A new hospital, opened by Her Majesty the Queen on 8 August 1985, has replaced the five former hospitals in the town. The Royal Highland Yacht Club and the Oban Sailing Club are both based in the town. Sailing around the Hebrides is still regarded as heaven as the waters are unspoiled and the islands provide excellent hostelries. A new facility for short-stay yachtsmen is in the process of being developed between Oban's North and South Piers. The lifeboat, one of the six RNLI boats stationed in Argyll, is berthed at Port Beg, on the south side of the harbour.

Oban, now known as the crossroads of the Highlands and the Isles, is the terminal of the ferries to the Inner and Outer Hebrides. The Caledonian MacBrayne fleet contributes not only to the wealth of the town, but provides essential services to the islanders as well as transport for hundreds of thousands of visitors who take 'The Sea Road to the Isles'.

Recently Oban has become a university town with the granting of a Royal Charter to the University of the Highlands and Islands. The Marine Biodiversity Laboratory at Dunstaffnage is a full academic partner, having the power to grant degrees in marine science in its own right. The development at SAMS (Scottish Association of Marine Science) now employs around 180 people and is one of the town's major employers. A science park is to be developed alongside, bringing further high-quality employment. Oban is the birthplace of An Comunn Gaidhealach, the leading organisation in the promotion of the Gaelic language through the Royal National Mod. It is known worldwide for its high standard of competitive solo piping: to win the Gold Medal at the Argyllshire Gathering, held annually at the end of August, is one of the highest accolades that can be achieved.

## Lochgilphead

Circa 1750 there was one small house or farm on the north shore of Lochgilp. By 1800 some houses had been built by John MacNeill of Gigha on his Oakfield estate and others were then erected by Peter Campbell of Kilmory. During the first half of the 19th century the town continued to develop. The population rose steadily as people, driven off the land by sheep farming, found a living in fishing.

The establishment of a regular steamboat service between Glasgow and Ardrishaig, which began in the 1820s, meant that fresh fish, caught in Loch Fyne, could be sent to the Glasgow market. Larger boats with lug sails, introduced by Ayrshire fishermen, could trail up to 300 nets behind them. Also the old practice of tanning nets with bark was abandoned for the use of catechu. Herring, cod and ling were the main catches and by 1844 a total of 108 boats were crewed by 326 men and boys while 167 other people were employed in gutting and packing. Smoked fish and herring salted in barrels were also popular and seven coopers and four curers found themselves fully employed.

A distillery, sited on the Crinan Canal, closed early in the 20th century and gasworks provided lighting before the introduction of electricity.

Kilmory Castle, to the south-east of Lochgilphead, was built in the early 19th century by the Campbells of Kilmory. Subsequently it was enlarged into a baronial mansion by Sir John Powlett Orde Bt. on the plans of the English architect J G Davis, and later additions, in 1878, completed its present form. Sir John, renowned as an eccentric, became unpopular after an accident involving his coach resulted in the death of a child. Subsequently, c1830, he devised a scheme to build a causeway across the head of Loch Gilp in order to be able to cross it without going into the town. The now largely ruinous building, with a high pitched roof known as the Clock Lodge, on the roadside below the castle, marks the north end of the intended route. However the fishermen, furious at his interference, breached the stonework, remains of which are still visible at low tide.

Four walnut trees were planted, one at each corner of the town, probably by the Campbells of Kilmory or else by the Powlett Ordes. Today one survivor remains by the bank of the burn that runs beneath a bridge immediately beyond the roundabout on the southern approach to Lochgilphead.

Prior to the passing of the Poor Law (Scottish) Amendment Act of 1845, which made the Parish responsible for dispensing and supplying medicine to the sick and the poor, the lairds were largely responsible for the welfare of those on their estates. There were, however, three doctors in Lochgilphead in 1831. Archibald Currie's book on North Knapdale, written in 1830, describes how:

> The traveler approaches the Crinan Canal, on the north side of which is Carnban, the friendly dwelling of Dr MacCallum. Here he may have it in his power to taste of mountain dew in its purity, for it is here refined by being kept for years in the house, some of which is mixed with juniper berries, some with chamomile flowers, and such other medicinal ingredients that are conductive to health. As the Doctor is a facetious man, and full of diverting anecdotes, the traveler will be pleasantly amused with his jocose and fanciful description of men and manners.

Another anecdote, in similar vein, concerns Doctor MacLeod of Tayvallich, the village on the single-track road which runs south from Crinan to the point of Keilmore some 20 miles south-west of Lochgilphead in Knapdale. Being not fully qualified, he could not be appointed Parochial Medical Officer but the neighbouring doctors, together with the rest of the population, had every confidence in his ability. He looked after the sick in Tayvallich and district and on the island of Jura, and lived until about 1890. His cottage, called Tigh-an-Leigh (the Doctor's House), was almost opposite the site of the present Post Office. The area on the opposite side of the road, enclosed by a stone dyke and now partly occupied by the village shop, is referred to in the Tayvallich Estate titles as Doctor MacLeod's Garden.

Amongst many stories about him is one concerning an incident after he had retired. His legs by then had given out to the point where he could barely walk. Nonetheless, one goodwife in Tayvallich, who was about to give birth, would have none other than Doctor MacLeod to attend her. Accordingly her husband got out the big manure barrow, wheeled it to the village, loaded the doctor onto it, wrapped him up well with coat and muffler and wheeled him up and down the hill the one and a half miles to Tayvullin.

Then after the child was safely delivered he wheeled the doctor home again.

In 1858 the General Board of Commissioners in Lunacy for Scotland was formed, and the Asylum in Lochgilphead opened in 1863. The Argyll and Bute Hospital, as this was to become known, was rebuilt on an adjoining site in 2006. The Mid-Argyll Hospital, sited next to the Poor House, was built in 1896 at an estimated cost of £1,084, the successful contractor being Mr Hugh McAlpine, Drimvore. The hospital, built of corrugated iron, with room for up to 14 patients, opened in the following year. When the National Health Service began in 1948, it was classified as an Infectious Diseases Hospital of 12 beds. By then the building was dilapidated and a new hospital was built on the same site in 1959.

In 1974, on the formation of three-tier local government, Kilmory Castle became the headquarters of Argyll and Bute District Council, which became Argyll and Bute Council in 1996. A separate modern block was built in 1982 and the main house was restored after a fire in 1983.

The Mid Argyll swimming pool, 20 metres in length, was opened in 1998. Although acknowledged as a great amenity, the struggle to maintain it financially remains an ongoing problem.

## Tarbert

The little town of Tarbert clusters round the harbour where the longboats lay at anchor in the days of the Norse invasion. Tarbert means 'tow-boat', and galleys were towed on rollers from East to West Loch Tarbert, thus giving the town its name.

Tarbert Harbour, at the head of an inlet of Loch Fyne, has been known throughout the centuries as one of the most sheltered anchorages on Scotland's west coast. Much used by yachtsmen during the summer, it is also a base for fishing boats throughout the year. The registration number of local boats are prefixed with the letters TB. Fishing remains the chief industry. There are five fish processing factories and four huge lorries, loaded with live shellfish, go out to Barcelona each week.

Tarbert Castle, rebuilt in the 14th century as a Royal Castle by Robert the Bruce, as is proved by the Scottish Exchequer Rolls, is currently being renovated with the help of grants. Much of the work of preservation, however, is being done by members of the

Tarbert Conservation Initiative, and the Skipness Community Trust, owner of the Royal Castle today. Ground around the site of the castle, with the assistance of the Forestry Commission, is being cleared and the Kintyre Way Path, badly eroded, is being improved. When finished the castle and its environment will become of increasing interest as one of the most important places in Argyll.

## Campbeltown

Campbeltown was founded in 1609 by Archibald, 7th Earl of Argyll. He was then settling Lowland families in the district and built the castle of Lochhead, on the site of the Castlehill Church, to protect the surrounding area. The former Castlehill Church has now been converted into flats.

Campbeltown, already an important fishing port, was created a Royal Burgh in 1700. Later it became famous for its whisky and, in the latter part of the 19th century, it contained no less than 34 distilleries. Today the Springbank Distillery is the only one still in production. The oldest family-owned distillery in Scotland, it produces whisky under several well-known labels, all of which are very successful.

Another main industry is the Campbeltown Creamery. Founded in the early 1900s, on the site of two former distilleries, it was privately converted into a cheese manufacturing facility. At that time milk was brought in primarily to make sweet condensed milk and skimmed milk powder, but in the late 1970s the machinery was converted to produce cheese. In 1991–92 the total output amounted to 38,718 million litres of milk, which, coming mostly from local farms, gave 4,006 tons of dairy produce, figures which remained an average assessment over the last 20 years. The business, which employs 29 people, makes a variety of award-winning cheddars. Entries to the International Cheese Awards since 2007 have culminated in a gold and a silver medal in 2010.

In July 2009 plans were drawn up to build a new state-of-the-art creamery at Snipefield, on the outskirts of Campbeltown. Planning permission has been given, the present Creamery having been bought by Tesco for the erection of a new superstore on the site. A factory which began making sports jackets in 1955 was taken over by Jaeger in 1977. This firm, which employed 200 people and had an annual turnover of approximately £6.5 million, sadly went into liquidation.

The statue of Highland Mary, Dunoon

The buildings are now demolished. Likewise the Campbeltown Shipyard, started in 1968 at Trench Point, which specialised in building fishing boats and employed 70 men, has now also been closed.

In 2003 Vestas, a Danish company, established with state assistance a £10-million wind turbine manufacturing plant on part of the former RAF Machrihanish site. The workforce was over 100 strong but it closed its operation in 2008. The business was taken over by another Danish company, Skycon, again with government assistance. In 2010 Skycon and its parent company went into administration thus putting the future of the 120 jobs at Machrihanish into a state of uncertainty. However, in May 2011, Wind Tower Ltd completed the joint venture between Scottish & Southern Energy plc and Marsh Wind Technology Ltd in the purchase of the Skylon Wind Turbine.

The airport for Campbeltown is Machrihanish, some three 3 km west of the town. Loganair, operating first on behalf of British Airways and now for Flybe, runs twice daily services to and from Glasgow Airport. The RAF base at Machrihanish has been closed for some years. It stands adjacent to the championship golf course, which lies above the great sweep of sand around the crescent of Machrihanish Bay. There is some hope that a community buyout will acquire the site for industrial, commercial and community purposes. A new private golf course has been built at Machrihanish, adjacent to the existing course. It is being extensively marketed. The ferry service to Northern Ireland lasted only three years. A long campaign for its reinstatement appears to have failed.

On the positive side, the local authority has built a very fine swimming pool, library and gymnasium. Situated on Kinloch Green, it is called Aqualibrium.

## Dunoon

Dunoon, on the north side of the Clyde Estuary, is built round the East and West Bays, which are divided by the headland of Castle Hill.

The ruins of Dunoon Castle surmount the top of the hill. In 1334, when seized by the English, it was re-taken by Sir Colin Campbell of Loch Awe, who then was made Hereditary Governor, a title which remains with the Duke of Argyll. In 1563 Mary, Queen of Scots, after leaving Inveraray and sailing across Loch Fyne, stayed here. Lower down on Castle Hill a statue of Burns' Highland Mary stands within view of Ayrshire, where she knew brief happiness with her lover.

During the 19th century, following the development of regular steamboat services in the Clyde, Dunoon developed as a holiday resort. The mansion house of Castle Toward, standing at the end of a peninsula, was built in 1832 by the then Lord Provost of Glasgow. Later it became a residential school, owned by the Glasgow Corporation, to which parties of Argyll children went for summer camps. It is currently being used as an outdoor centre.

Toward Castle, the former stronghold of the Lamonts (see p. 19), now ruined and overgrown with ivy, stands nearby within the grounds. The headquarters of the Argyll and Bute Library Services, based originally in Hunter Street, was moved to Highland Avenue c1996. The Cowal Highland Games, ending with the march of the thousand pipers, is a great annual event.

# CHAPTER 8: Islands of the Inner Hebrides – the Past and the Present

*Gigha*

The southernmost island of the Inner Hebrides, Gigha lies off the west coast of Kintyre, east of Islay. The name derives from the Norse worse Gudey, meaning 'Good Island' or 'God's Island'. Today about 110 people live there, compared to 600 in the 18th century. Archaeological remains prove that lying as it does on the sea route along the Kintyre Peninsula, it has been inhabited for as long as 5,000 years. In 1263 King Haakon of Norway anchored his fleet in the Sound of Gigha before his defeat at the Battle of Largs.

In the heart of the island the ruined Church of Kilchattan contains gravestones of great antiquity and, nearby, to the west, the Ogham Stone is engraved in the mysterious language of the Picts. Ownership of the island was complex until, in 1865, Captain William Scarlett bought it and built Achamore House. The famous garden planted by Sir James Horlick, a later laird, is described in the Garden Section of this book. Since 2002 the island has been owned through a development trust called the Isle of Gigha Heritage Trust. Ardminish, the only village on the island, is the terminus of the car ferry which runs to and from Tayinloan in Kintyre.

The small island of Cara, to the south of Gigha, has been uninhabited since the early 1940s. A sanctuary for gulls and other ground-nesting birds, it is also a haunt of otters and a flock of wild goats.

*Islay*

In 1725 the island of Islay was sold by the Campbells of Cawdor to Daniel Campbell of Shawfield, Great Daniel as he was known, a successful merchant in Glasgow. He died in 1753 and was succeeded by his grandson of the same name.

Daniel the Younger, greatly impressed by Italian architecture while making the Grand Tour, returned to design and build the model town of Bowmore.

The Round Church, at the top of the wide main street, was built for farm workers, fisher families and weavers at a time when Bowmore was renowned for its linen and woven cloth. Daniel the Younger, who promoted these industries, also built a distillery and organised the first weekly sailing packet between West Loch Tarbert and Islay. Today the Round Church and the model town remain as memorials to his enterprise.

The town of Port Ellen, around Leodamus Bay, in the south-east of the island, was founded by Walter Frederick Campbell of Islay in 1821 and named after Lady Elinor Charteris, his first wife. Port Charlotte, also founded by him, is called after his mother, Lady Charlotte Campbell, a daughter of the Duke of Argyll. It was laid out in 1828. Both towns were designed as centres for local industries, agriculture, distilling, and fishing. Later, in 1833, Walter Frederick also began building the small fishing village of Port Wemyss, near Portnahaven, founded by his uncle, Captain Walter Campbell of Sunderland, *c*1830.

In 1853 the Campbells of Shawfield sold Islay to the Morrisons, ancestors of Lord Margadale, the largest landowner today. Subsequently, in 1855, the Morrisons sold the Kildalton estate in the south of the island to the Ramsays (the present owner is Sir Ian MacTaggart) and the Dunlossit Estate to Sir Smith Child (it now belongs to the Scroders) as well as other parts of their land. Dunlossit Estate has its own abattoir, the one in Ballygrant having closed.

Leaving Port Askaig, Jura in the distance

The cheese factory, for which Islay was once famous, has now closed. Sadly this means that many of the herds of cattle, particularly of the Ayrshire breed, such a lovely sight when out at grass, have now gone. The wool mill, however, continues to produce beautiful tartan and tweed. Amongst new developments is a soap-making business in Bowmore called Spirited Soaps. Also, in Islay House Square, is a chocolate maker worthy of note. Of particular interest to visitors is the new community centre and camp site at Port Charlotte, called Port Mor. Community owned, it uses renewable energy for all forms of light and heating.

Distilling remains the main industry and, although the number is reduced, nine distilleries still produce the world-famous Islay whisky today. Coincidentally, the Laggan Distillery, at Port Ellen, looks across at the ruins of Dunyvaig Castle where Coll Ciotach MacDonald so famously demanded a bottle of his favourite *aqua vitae* before surrendering to Campbell of Dunstaffnage in 1647. How convenient would the proximity of his favourite tipple have been to him had it existed in his day!

More recently the farm-based Kilchoman Distillery was opened in 2006, while among other new enterprises is the brewery at Bridgend.

Far from being an outpost, Islay is now in the forefront of conversion of natural sources into energy. The Islay Energy Trust, funded by the Scottish Government's Climate Challenge Fund, has worked with households on the island to cut bills and improve energy efficiency. The focus for the new project – RACES (Renewables and Carbon/Energy Savings) – will offer the same support to small businesses, while further exploring the scope for community renewables on the island. The last is vital if Islay Energy Trust is to become a self-sustaining organisation, and also to meet the aim of developing a community trust for the benefit of the island.

The Limpet Wave Station near Portnahaven has proved to be a successful test bed for wave technology and has been used as a prototype for the much larger wave power station that is planned for Siadar on Lewis.

Making headline news is the proposed use of the tides, surging between Islay and Jura, to produce electricity. The Sound of Islay Tidal Energy project, with the proposal for a 10MW tidal energy array in the Sound, has reached another milestone with the announcement by the Scottish Government that it has given consent to Scottish Power Renewables (SPR) to proceed. This is the world's first tidal energy array to be given consent and if testing proves successful in Orkney 10x1MW devices will be installed just south of Port Askaig in the summer of 2013.

Scotland has over 25 per cent of Europe's tidal energy potential and some of the best locations are around Islay. The proposed Scottish Power Renewables project in the Sound of Islay could provide the equivalent of the electricity used by 5,000 homes.

With a population of only 3,500, the small community of Islay is becoming increasingly important as a source of renewable energy.

*Jura*

People are believed to have lived on Jura as long as 7,000 years ago, in the caves on the raised beaches on the west coast. The island was called Dyr oe (pronounced Joorah), meaning 'Deer Island', by the Vikings who probably overcame the earlier people.

It is almost divided by an isthmus at Tarbert, the name being an indication that boats were dragged from shore to shore. The three cone-shaped mountains, known as the Paps of Jura, are the most outstanding feature. Rising to over 2,000 feet they dominate the landscape even when seen from afar. The highest is called Beinn an Oir, the Hill of Gold, because traditionally treasure lies buried close by.

Jura was once a part of the Lordship of the Isles, but following the defeat of the MacDonalds in 1615, the island was forfeited by the Crown and a charter of Jura was granted to the Earl of Argyll. In 1666 Duncan, a younger son of Alexander Campbell, 3rd of Lochnell, received the lands of Sanaig, in Jura, from the 9th Earl who appointed him as baillie and chamberlain of the island.

Pennant in his Tour, written in 1769, described the shielings of people who kept a herd of goats. He said they were built of wattle, similar to the tepees of the American Indians, rather than of stone. Within were dairy utensils and baskets to hold cheese.

Cattle rearing at that time was the island's main concern. The harbour of Lagg on Jura, some eight miles to the north-east of Craighouse, was the main embarkation point for the great herds of animals that were shipped across the Sound of Jura to Keills, in Knapdale, on the mainland. From here went not only the Jura cattle, but those from Islay and Colonsay, first transported to Jura, en route to the mainland. Piers for both terminals were designed in 1806 by David Wilson, a Lochgilphead surveyor, whose plans were then altered by James Hollinsworth, and the estimated cost at Lagg rose to £317. 6s. 4d. Archibald Campbell of Jura undertook the contract, and work on the piers, begun in 1809, finished within two years. The Keills–Lagg ferry became the postal route for mail and an extension of the road to Tarbert was made in 1814.

Plans to re-establish this route as the main link with Islay and Jura, which have been considered recently, have so far failed to materialise. Jura is now reached most easily by the ferry service of Caledonian MacBrayne which lands at Port Askaig, from where a smaller ferry plies back and forth across the Sound of Islay to a pier on Jura's west shore. The pier at Craighouse, the main village which lies at the south-east end of the island, was built by the Commissioners for the Highland Roads and Bridges between 1812 and 1814 at the cost of £712.

A distillery was reopened here by Scottish & Newcastle Breweries in the late 1950s, largely thanks to the enterprise of the late Sir William Younger.

The land which was once good cattle ground is still partly farmed, but deer, as in the days of the

The Paps of Jura

Norsemen, remain the predominant species. Strangely, in view of its ancient habitation, Jura is one of the least populated areas of Europe. Although as the crow flies it is only 50 miles from Glasgow, its population of only just over 200 people is greatly exceeded by that of red deer.

The famous whirlpool of Corrievreckan, feared by seamen through the centuries, lies between the north-west end of Jura and the nearby island of Scarba. The turbulence caused by the meeting of tides above a subterranean reef gave rise to the ancient belief of it being a cauldron in which the Cailleach of Cruachan washed her clothes.

## Colonsay and Oronsay

Colonsay, even at the time of the first settlers, is thought to have been two islands, for what is now Kiloran Glen was once a channel of the sea.

For many years it was accepted that the islands were named in honour of St Columba and St Oran but the origins of the names have recently been classified. In Lake Vänem in Sweden the island of Kallândso is pronounced Colbhasa. It was the site of the last battle ever fought in Scandinavia by Magnus Barelegs. The island has a smaller pendicle called Orensö (pronounced Orasa), which means tidal island, therefore the Norsemen may have transferred the names. An alternative theory, however, might be that the name derives from the old Gaelic word Coll, meaning hazelwood island.

The smaller island of Oronsay (undoubtedly a Norse name), joined by a causeway at ebb tide, lies off the southern end of Colonsay. A Christian community is believed to have been established there soon after the foundation of Iona, and the ruins of the 16th-century priory contain some of the finest examples of the work of the sculptors believed to have come from Iona.

Both islands have been long inhabited because of the fertility of their soil. The remains of a substantial encampment found at Loch Staosnaig in Colonsay are over 6,000 years old. They show signs of sophisticated activity, including post holes for various structures, a substantial pit and arrangements for the processing of both lesser celandine and hazelnuts on a prodigious scale. Stones found in the sand in Oronsay have been proved by carbon dating to have been used, probably as part of a cooking hearth, during the Mesolithic Age, perhaps about 5,000 BC, and the Mesolithic shell-mounds of Oronsay are quite prominent and date from about that time. The first recorded inhabitants, following Somerled's conquest of the Isles, were the MacDuffies, or MacPhees, a clan of great antiquity traditionally descended from a mermaid. Following their ascendancy, in the 13th and 14th centuries, the MacDuffies became hereditary archivists of the MacDonalds of the Isles.

In 1588 Mary Queen of Scots granted Colonsay to Sir James MacDonald, 6th of Dunyvaig, and he then transferred it to his brother Coll Maol Dubh, grandfather of Coll Ciotach.

The house of the MacDonalds of Colonsay, called An Sabhal Ban (The White Barn) stood close to Kiloran Bay. It is thought to have been near to the site of the present Colonsay House which dates from 1722. Colonsay by then belonged to the MacNeills, who bought it in 1701 from the 1st Duke of Argyll.

The house that they built, consisting of two storeys, a cellar and an attic, survives as the central block of Colonsay House. Major alterations, carried out in the first half of the 19th century, included the additions of the two pavilions with Palladian windows, which are linked to the north-facing front of the house by corridors and a single block (later raised to two floors) at the back.

The island was bought by the 1st Lord Strathcona and Mount Royal in 1904. He made further alterations to the house and also began the garden in the natural shelter of the glen. Many of the more tender varieties of plants thrive there, including the lovely magnolias which are such a feature in the spring.

Scalasaig, the only village on Colonsay, is distinguished by a beautiful early 19th-century parish church. It also has a comfortable and well designed hotel run today by the Colonsay Estate. Mr Kevin Byrne and his wife Christa, previous owners of the hotel, in 1995 acquired the publishing business of House of Lochar in partnership with Miss Georgina Hobhouse, who has lived most of her life on Colonsay and Oronsay where her family once farmed. Their books are largely focused on Scotland and this enterprise brings a new aspect to the life of this beautiful Hebridean island.

Other flourishing businesses today include an oyster farm and apiary founded by Andrew Abrahams, who has restored a major colony of the native Scottish bee. The island is also home to the award-winning Colonsay Brewery, founded by Chris Nisbet and Rob Pocklington.

In recent years the community purchased some hundreds of acres of land and has established six new crofts to attract new families to the island. The island of Oronsay has had the benefit of major investment in its infrastructure and is currently leased to the RSPB as a sanctuary, with the farm being managed to enhance the habitat.

*The Isles of Mull*

Mull is an island of mountains which sweep down towards the sea. Ben More, the mightiest, reaches 3,162 feet.

Mull in the 13th century was part of the island possessions of the MacDougalls of Lorn, but King Robert the Bruce awarded it to Angus MacDonald of Islay and Kintyre following his conquest of Argyll. Later it came into the possession of the MacLeans of Duart until acquired in 1674 by the 9th Earl of Argyll.

Duart Castle, garrisoned until 1751, was then left roofless and abandoned. But in 1911 the by then ruinous castle was bought by Sir Fitzroy MacLean, 25th of Duart, from the Murray Guthries. Sir Fitzroy then immediately commissioned the Glasgow architect Sir John Burnet to restore and rebuild the castle and

Tobermory

added the beautiful Sea Room with its view of the Sound of Mull.

The castle, which is open to the public, is now the home of Sir Lachlan MacLean Bt., 18th chief of Clan MacLean. Dun Ara, positioned to protect the central stretch of the Sound of Mull, was a stronghold of the MacKinnons, thought to have held lands in Mull from c1354. Moy Castle, attributed to the brother of Hector MacLean of Duart, progenitor of the family of MacLean of Lochbuie, was sited to defy invaders at the head of Lochbuie. Abandoned c1752 in favour of a more comfortable house, it is said to be haunted by a headless horseman on dark and windy nights.

Tobermory, one of the finest natural harbours on the west coast, was chosen by the British Fisheries Society as the site of a new settlement in 1787. The substantial slated houses built round the waterfront included an inn, designed by Robert Mylne, the architect of much of Inveraray, and a custom house and collector's lodging. Rows of cottages above, planned mainly for the fisher families, have since been largely rebuilt. The Stevenson brothers of Oban were the main contractors. Ships of large tonnage were increasing and the pier, which went deep enough to allow them to come aside, was built in 1814.

A distillery, opened in 1820, after several closures is once again in production. Its famous Tobermory whisky is renowned throughout the world.

Today, as the principal town of Mull, Tobermory has many visitors. The harbour, home of the Western Isles Sailing Club, remains a venue for yachtsmen. The climax of the season comes in July when, as the Firth of Clyde–Tobermory Regatta takes place, many boats under sail converge upon the sheltered harbour.

Craignure in the south-east of the island has been the main point of arrival and departure since the car ferry service began in 1964. From there a double road runs only to Salen – an extension to Tobermory is under way – but elsewhere in the island there are only single-track roads which are rapidly proving inadequate for the ever-increasing amount of traffic today.

Mull was one of the places most affected by the introduction of sheep during the last century when many people left the island to find work elsewhere. Sheep farming is still a main industry and there are many cattle on the island, mostly of Highland or cross Highland breeds. The Highland Fold at Glengorm, on the north-east coast, is internationally known.

During the 1950s Glenforsa Estate, near Salen, was acquired by the Department of Agriculture and Fisheries and run as a single sheep farm. Now divided into two units it is leased to local men. Other holdings in the island, owned by the State and rented by the Department, have largely been sold to the sitting tenants during the last two decades. The village of

Dervaig in the north of the island was laid out as a planned village by the then landlord, Maclean of Coll, in 1799. Today, despite modern innovations, it retains its old-world charm.

Mull is becoming increasingly well known as a developing centre of the arts. There are many artists and craftsmen living and working on the island and their work can be viewed in various shops, galleries, and open workshops/studios. An Tobar, the Tobermory Art Centre, which opened in 1997, holds exhibitions of local, national and international work and has become known for presenting quality traditional and modern Scottish music. An Tobar supplies a leaflet listing all the artists and craft workers and their addresses on the island. The newly opened Visitor Centre at Fionnphort is also of great interest particularly for the many visitors to Iona (described in the section devoted to churches in this book).

The Mull Little Theatre, which was founded by the enterprising incomers Barry and Marianne Hesketh, has moved from its original small venue in Dervaig to purpose-built premises just outside of Tobermory. It is now known as Mull Theatre and has a national reputation.

## The Islands off the Coast of Mull

### Inchkenneth

Inchkenneth lies a short way off the west coast of Mull. It takes its name from St Cainneach, or Kenneth, a fellow student of St Columba at the monastery of St Finian at Clonard.

During the 15th century Inchkenneth was appropriated by the Augustinian nunnery of Iona, but in 1574, following the Reformation, the last prioress of Iona surrendered the island to Hector MacLean of Duart.

The 13th-century chapel, now ruinous, stands on the east side of the island above a sandy beach where boats can easily land. The close associations with Iona are revealed in the beautiful carving of medieval grave slabs within the church and the church-yard. Most are memorials to the MacLeans of Duart, owners of the island from the 14th century until 1674, when it became the property of the 9th Earl of Argyll.

Doctor Johnson and James Boswell visited Inchkenneth in 1773 when they stayed with Sir Allan MacLean of Duart, who then leased Inchkenneth from the Duke of Argyll. Johnson wrote afterwards that 'We could easily have been persuaded to stay longer upon Inch Kenneth, but life will not all be passed in delight.'

Sometime between 1837 and 1846 Lieut-Colonel Robert MacDonald, son of MacDonald of Boisdale, bought Inchkenneth and built 'a neat new mansion'. There were then 100 inhabitants, many of them soldiers returned from the European wars. In 1847 when the potato famine was at its worst, the island was ploughed from end to end to keep the people alive. MacDonald gave financial help to emigrants, finally ruining himself to the point where he also had to leave.

Inchkenneth was then bought by the Clarks of Ulva, in whose time the mansion house was almost destroyed by fire. It was rebuilt by a Mrs Malloch in 1890.

Later owners included Lord Redesdale, whose daughter, Unity Mitford, was a devotee of Adolf Hitler. Jessica Redesdale sold Inchkenneth to the late Doctor Barlow and his wife in 1967. It is now owned by Professor Martin Barlow and his sister Doctor Claire Barlow, who while based in England, come as often as possible to this otherwise uninhabited island.

### Ulva

Ulva is the hereditary island of the MacQuarries. The old chief entertained Doctor Johnson and Boswell in 1773 in the old house, now partly incorporated in farm buildings. A few years later he sold the island to MacDonald of Boisdale, who greatly developed the kelp industry to the point where it produced no less than 4% of all the kelp in the Highlands.

Sadly he had already sold out to Mr F.W. Clark, a solicitor from Stirling, when the trade failed. The potato blight struck in 1847, and the people faced destitution. The new proprietor, unlike his neighbour on Inchkenneth, apparently showed little compassion and turned the island into a sheep run thus forcing people to leave. The population fell from 500 to a mere 150 in only four years. Today there are only about 11 people left. Ulva House, built by MacDonald of Staffa *c*1790, was destroyed by fire in 1954. It was rebuilt by Lady Congleton, whose descendants, the Howards, live there throughout the year.

The smaller island of Gometra, joined to the west of Ulva by a bridge, was also denuded by the potato famine despite the efforts of the Miss MacDonalds, the then owners, to provide work on the island. As on neighbouring Ulva, traces of old cottages tell their own sad tale.

## Staffa

Staffa, a small uninhabited island which lies to the south-west of Gometra, became famous in 1772 when Sir Joseph Banks, president of the Royal Society, first informed the world of the wonders of the grotto on the south side of the island which is known as Fingal's Cave. Early travellers who visited it included the French geographer Faujas St Fond. More famously, in 1828 the German composer Felix Mendelssohn came on the newly established steamer service to visit the cave. The voyage was extremely rough but the surge of the waves into the echoing cavern inspired him to write the evocative overture *Fingal's Cave*. Back then there were goats on Staffa but now just a few sheep remain. They graze round the ruins of a few cottages now empty for 200 years.

## The Treshnish Islands

The Treshnish Islands, rich in historical interest and the home of countless birds, are the most outlying islands off the west coast of Mull. Once they formed the demarcation line between the domains of Somerled and his successors and those of the King of Norway, until in 1266 the Norwegians, following the defeat of their King Haakon, ceded their Hebridean islands to Alexander III in return for a promised rent.

The islands of Carnburg Mor and Carnburg Beag, divided by a tidal channel, are the most northerly of the chain. In 1343 they were granted to John I, Lord of the Isles, by King David II. Ruins of a fortress and of a chapel remain on Carnburg Mor.

The fortress, perched high above the sea, must have been virtually impregnable. The natural rock was enforced with stone to make an encircling wall which was pierced with loop holes through which weapons could be fired. It is known to have been garrisoned during the Civil War until about 1649. Ruins of defences can also be traced on Carnburg Beag.

To the south-west lies Fladday, and the long island of Lunga where stones of old houses remain. The most outlying island of all is Bac Mor, known as

the Dutchman's Cap because of its resemblance to a flat crowned hat. Here except on the calmest days it is almost impossible to land, yet traces of habitation can be seen from the sea and it is thought that the people of the other islands may at one time have used it for summer grazing.

## Coll

Coll, to the north-west of Mull, is a long reef just two miles across at its widest point. The only village is Arinagour, on an inlet on the south-east coast. It is a dynamic community with many young families, and its population has doubled in the past 40 years.

The early history of the island and of the old castle of Breachachadh has already been described in the section of this book concerning medieval castles. The New Castle, which stands adjacent to the old, was built by Hector MacLean, 13th of Coll, in 1750. Doctor Johnson, who stayed here three years later, during his Hebridean Tour, referred to it contemptuously as 'a neat villa, a mere tradesman's box with nothing of the chief about it'.

In 1856 John Lorne Stewart, chamberlain of the Argyll Estates in Kintyre, bought the island from the MacLeans. Stewart, who was a progressive farmer, introduced dairy herds. He also brought in families from Ayrshire to teach local people how to make cheese. Their descendants live there today.

The island is a haunt of seabirds and countless Atlantic seals, which bask in sunlight on the rocks. Away from the shore on open moorland red-throated divers, greylag geese and red-necked phalarope are amongst the many birds which nest near the freshwater lochs. Coll is also one of the last breeding places of corncrakes, and recently when Mr Kenneth Stewart sold the Coll Estate, the RSPB bought some of the south-west end of the island to give sanctuary to these now very rare birds. Their numbers are now much increased.

The Old Castle of Breachachadh, by then entirely ruined, was sold by Mr Kenneth Stewart to Major Nicholas MacLean Bristol in 1967. Nick Bristol, who had already formed the Project Trust, moved to Coll permanently in 1972.

Breachachadh Castle has now been the Trust's headquarters for over 20 years. Project now has its own specially built premises, consisting of a 40-bed Selection and Training Centre and offices renovated

Sorrisdale, Coll

from the old farmhouse of Ballyhough, renamed the Hebridean Centre.

The Trust's aim is to educate a new generation of young people in Europe through service in partnership with people overseas, particularly in developing countries. It uses the island as a model to help volunteers understand a different community when they go overseas.

The Project Trust, with a staff of 21, is the largest single employer on Coll. Currently 260 volunteers are working in 20 different countries and the Trust is known internationally for the wide scope of its achievements. It has now sent more than 6,000 volunteers overseas.

## Tiree

Both Coll and Tiree, which lies further to the west, have some of the finest beaches in the world. Shell sand, ground by the Atlantic breakers, lies silver under the sun. The shallow sea is emerald and then as the depth increases, it changes through shades of blue to the beautiful but sinister purple which indicates dangerous reefs.

Because of its low altitude, which does not attract rain, it has more hours of sunshine than anywhere else in Great Britain. Thanks to its dry climate, which favours the growth of corn, Coll was known in the days of St Columba as the Granary of the Isles.

Tiree belongs to the trustees of the 10th Duke of Argyll. The Island House was built by the 3rd Duke as a house for his factor in 1748. Despite some 19th-century additions it has retained its character and is now one of the family homes of the present Duke and his family. In 1982 the Hebridean Trust was founded under the leadership of the Stanfield family who have long-standing connections with Tiree. It was formed as an educational trust to develop projects, which will bring enduring cultural as well as economic benefits to the island communities of the Hebrides. Most of the Trust's major projects have so far been based on Tiree, but plans exist for expansion on some other islands.

In 1984 the old Signal Tower of Hynish, which formerly relayed messages to the Skerryvore Lighthouse lying out in the ocean off the south-west tip of Tiree, was turned into Skerryvore Museum. It records the design and construction of the lighthouse by Alan Stevenson, uncle of the author Robert Louis Stevenson, in the 1840s. In 1988 the Trust acquired the Old Storerooms, now called the Alan Stevenson House, which provides children, who might otherwise not have a holiday, with a chance to discover Tiree. The house is also rented to groups who do courses on a wide range of subjects and is thus self-supporting. Tiree has a population of approximately 780 people and it also has many visitors. There is now an air service from Oban two days a week.

The island is farmed largely by crofters, who, like most other islanders, rely on the ferries to bring in fodder and to transport their animals to the mainland sales. The ferry pier is at Scarinish on the south side of Gott Bay.

Tiree Rural Centre was opened in 2002, primarily to replace the old auction mart. Five sales are held each year where crofters can market their livestock. The centre also has a tearoom, internet access, office space and a cinema called the Ringside Theatre, which utilises the auction mart ring. Interpretation boards in the building introduce visitors to the rich environment of the island and tell how crofting is of key importance in supporting the environment.

An Talla opened in 2004 and was built on the site of the old hall. Youth groups meet here and dances and community events are held throughout the year.

Tiree Community Development Trust was formed in 2006 and is owned and managed by Tiree's community. It represents a community-led approach to rural development promoting the sustainable, environmental, economic and social development of Tiree.

On the economic side Tiree Renewable Energy Ltd is a wholly owned subsidiary of Tiree Development Trust. TREL built and operate a wind turbine on the island to finance community projects.

Tiree Array, a very large offshore wind farm, is being planned for the area around the Skerryvore Lighthouse. It could provide more than one fifth of Scotland's electricity needs. Tiree Development Trust is actively involved in representing Tiree's interests. Feis Thiriodh is a week-long festival held in July to celebrate the island's culture. Classes are run for both young and old and evenings are filled with dances, ceilidhs, lectures and walks.

Tiree Music Festival started in 2010 and is a two-day open-air Celtic music event in July for all ages. The Agricultural Show is also held in July, a family day out, held in the grounds of the Rural Centre. Tiree's Wave Classic windsurfing event is held in October.

## Lismore

The island of Lismore lies in Loch Linnhe, north-east of Mull. Mesolithic cairns prove early habitation. Tirfuir Broch is thought to have been built by the Picts. They were probably driven out by invading Norsemen, who constructed the fort of Castle Coeffin, on the north coast, with its tidal fish trap in the rocks below.

The fertile soil, composed almost entirely of Dalradian limestone, so famously referred to by St Moluag, gave the island the Gaelic name meaning great garden. Famous for cattle breeding, it was also highly cultivated when people lived almost entirely off the land.

In 1845 the population numbered 1430, although the census shows that less than 30 years later, in 1871, there were only 180, many having gone to find work on the mainland or emigrated abroad.

The island is linked to the mainland by two ferries, a roll-on roll-off from Oban and a foot ferry, which takes bicycles, from Port Appin to the north end of the island. Lismore Lighthouse, built by Robert Stevenson, stands on the small island of Eilean Musdile to the south-west of Lismore. A well known landmark nearby is the skerry, known even more famously as the Lady's Rock.

Notoriously, in 1527, Lachlan MacLean, chief of the MacLeans of Duart, tried to murder his wife by leaving her there to drown, when the rock would be covered at high tide. Having sent a message to her brother, Archibald Campbell, 4th Earl of Argyll, telling of her sad demise, he then turned up at Inveraray Castle weeping crocodile tears. Taken in to the dining room, whom should he see to his horror, but his wife, sitting at the head of the table, very much alive.

It transpired she had been rescued by fishermen, who had passed the rock only just in time. MacLean left the castle unscathed but later was murdered in Edinburgh by Sir John Campbell of Calder, brother of his ill-treated wife.

Tales of the island's history are now kept safe for posterity in the Lismore Heritage Centre. Opened in March 2007, it is managed by the Comann Eachdreidh Lios Mòr Society, created in 1995 by Gaelic-speaking islanders specifically to record information that was in danger of being lost to future generations if not written down. The Society worked to create a centre in which the data they had collected could be stored. The Heritage Centre, which opens from March to October, is run entirely by volunteers. It comprises a museum, a room for archival storage and use of the curators, a library, which is also a public reference service, a gift shop and, last but not least, a café.

# CHAPTER 9: The Gardens

## INTRODUCTION

The first gardeners in Argyll seem to have been the Christian missionaries who began arriving in the 6th century AD. The Cistercian monks, in particular, were great horticulturists. They knew how to grow herbs and probably cultivated some vegetables.

Few people in the north-west of Scotland planted trees to enhance the landscape until the 17th century. The Marquis of Argyll began planting trees for amenity in the grounds of Inveraray Castle in the 1640s, But it was his son, the 9th Earl of Argyll, who, following the restoration of his estates, laid out the policies of Inveraray Castle between 1660 and 1680. His advisor was John Evelyn, one of the greatest silviculturists in the country. Some of the ancient trees in the beautiful avenue of limes, to the west of the castle, may be of his planting.

Trees, particularly sycamores, were planted for ornamental purposes round most of the houses built in the 18th century. Then in the early 19th century, botanists exploring abroad returned with seeds of many plants, which no one in this country had ever set eyes upon before.Sceptics declared they would die, killed by the poor soil and the cold, but astonishingly, thanks to the proximity of the Gulf Stream, it was found that plants from India, China, Tibet and countries in the Southern Hemisphere, could thrive in many places in Argyll.

The soil with its high proportion of peat is particularly suitable for rhododendrons, and areas of once bare hillside have now come alive with colour.It is however not only the great gardens, beautiful as they are, which make Argyll and the Islands so special for those who love plants. Many a cottage garden gladdens

the eye of passers by – the dahlias in a garden on the north-west approach to Oban, seem like a welcome to the town. Some of the smaller gardens in Taynuilt, and Easdale in Lorn and in Colintraive in Cowal, are now open concurrently in conjunction with the Scotland's Garden Scheme.

The first rhododendron to come to this country was the Alpine Rose R. Hirsutum which is known to have been flowering here in 1636. It survived because it is the only one of its species able to tolerate lime, which prevents the roots of others from absorbing nourishment from the soil.It was over a hundred years later, in 1763, when the mauve Rhododendron ponticumwas brought over here from the Caucasus. This glossy-leafed plant, which flowers most freely in June, now covers many hillsides in Argyll, and, with its vigorous growth, it is used as a stock plant for grafting other varieties.

In 1847, Sir Joseph Hooker, an eminent botanist, whose family had a small estate in Argyll, went plant hunting in the Sikkim Himalayas.There he found species of rhododendrons finer than any seen before. He returned home with seeds and fortunately gave some of them to the Campbells of Stonefield who were old family friends.

### Stonefield Castle, Tarbert

Designed by Sir William Playfair in 1837, Stonefield has now become a hotel and the gardens, although somewhat overgrown, still contain many Himalayan plants. Amongst rhododendrons discovered by Hooker, which grow here and elsewhere in Argyll, are R. thomsonii with its wonderful blood-red flowers, R. cinnabarinum, with greyish-green leaves and funnel-shaped flowers of bright cinnabar red, R. falconeri, which in contrast has creamy white and sometimes pale yellow blooms, with conspicuous dark purple splotches at the base, R. grande, with ivory white flowers, found by Hooker near Darjeeling, R. campylocarpum, with very strong yellow flowers, and R. triflorum, with its peeling red bark and faintly scented flowers which appear early in June.

## Crarae

The estate of Crarae, on the west coast of Loch Fyne, about one mile from Minard Village, was bought in 1825 by Sir Archibald Campbell of Succoth. However it was not until 1893 that Margaret, Lady Campbell, widow of the 4th Baronet, built Crarae Lodge on the site of an old inn. The garden was started about 1912 when Grace, wife of the 5th Baronet, was fired with enthusiasm by her nephew, Reginald Farrer, the traveller and plant collector, who, on expeditions to Kansu, in Western China in 1914 and to northern Burma in 1919, brought back many seeds to Crarae. An important development of this time was the planting of the mass of azaleas on the knoll known as Flagstaff Hill. Rhododendrons were planted amongst the magnificent European larches to the east side of the burn, R. falconeri, in particular, is covered each spring with trusses of cream-coloured flowers.

In 1925 Sir Archibald gave Crarae to his son, later Sir George Campbell, a passionate forester and gardener, who created the garden in the glen. The Crarae burn runs down the hill to Loch Fyne, over waterfalls and through pools, and in the sunlight the clear water above the bedrock is the colour of amber. Sir George laid out paths on each side of the burn from where one can appreciate the view of the shrubs and trees, well spaced out and in groups, Determined not to be enslaved by rhododendrons, he introduced species of trees and shrubs from all corners of the world.

There are twenty varieties of eucalyptus, mostly from Tasmania, the southern hemisphere beeches, (genus Nothofagus), the Dawn Redwood from China (Metasequoia glyptostroboides), and the Chilean Fire-bush (Embothrium longifolium). An abies grandis, brought by Sir George in a dog cart from Inveraray in 1908, when he was 14 years old, is now well over 100 feet high and native trees include some very fine Scots pines. Plants growing among the trees include magnolias, camellias, eucryphias, embothriums, clethras, malus (crab apple) and acers (maples), to name but a few. A great variety of primulas flower in spring and early summer and the blue poppy, mecanopsis, is as vivid as a kingfisher's wing.

Crarae, unlike most other gardens, stays open all the year round and the brilliance of spring flowering

Stonefield Castle Gardens

Achamore, Gigha

Much of the stone work came from Poltalloch House after it was demolished in 1958. Following her death the garden became overgrown until, in the 1970s, it was rescued by Mrs Robin Malcolm.

Despite the winds which strike the headland it is protected from storms, and plants from tropical countries flourish within the shelter of the glen. The garden is open from April to October and contributions to Action Aid can be left in the box at the gate. (Castle not open to the public).

## Achamore

The island of Gigha is reached by a car ferry from Tayinloan on the west coast of Kintyre. Achamore House and its 50 acres of garden lie within sheltering trees on the south-west end of the island. The house was built in 1884 and the garden was created by Sir James Horlick, 'the greatest plantsman of them all', between 1944 and 1973. The climate of Gigha is affected by the Gulf Stream, and the camellias and rare rhododendrons which grow there are rarely damaged by frost.

Many plants were bequeathed by Sir James Horlick to the National Trust and are now found in other gardens – notably Brodick on Arran – which belongs to the Trust in Scotland. The house is not open to the public.

## Arduaine

Arduaine takes its name from the green point on which it stands, on the south shore of Loch Melfort, some twenty miles (32km) south of Oban. In 1898 James Arthur Campbell, a retired tea planter from Ceylon, cruised around the West Coast of Scotland in search of a site on which to build a house and create a garden. From the sea he saw Arduaine, and knew that his quest was done. The Campbells took possession in 1905. The area round the house proved exposed to gales from the south and west so the garden was established near the shore, a short way to the west, where the absence of frost made it possible to grow the most tender species. Conifers and deciduous trees were then planted to give the framework for the enormous variety of plants for which Arduaine is so famous.

In 1971 the Campbells sold the garden to the brothers Mr Harry and Mr Eddie Wright, from Essex,

is hardly less exciting than that of the autumn colouring when deciduous trees stand out in radiant contrast against the more sombre conifers. Sir Ilay Campbell, who inherited the estate from his father in 1967, is one of the foremost horticulturists of the present day. In 1978 he transferred the larger part of the garden to the Crarae Gardens Charitable Trust for the benefit of the nation. (House not open to the public.)

## Duntrune Castle

The old garden of Duntrune, to the east of the castle, was restored by Mrs George Malcolm in the 1950s. Mrs Malcolm had at one time lived in Madeira and she designed this Scottish garden on the classical concept of some of the gardens she had seen there.

who restored it and altered its form. Arduaine has one of the best collections of rhododendrons in Scotland and amongst the most tender species are zeylanicum, the very rare R. nilagiricum, with its scarlet flowers, R. sinograndeand protistum (formerly R. giganteum) the first to flower in Great Britain. In 1992 the garden was generously presented to the National Trust by the Wrights.

## Achnacloich

Achnacloich, on the south-east shore of Loch Etive, is a garden which no-one should miss. It stands in an area of old woodland, where views of the mountains of Mull appear through gaps in the trees. The house dates from the 1840s, when the terraces, the walled garden and some of the woodland paths were begun. The family of Thomas Nelson & Sons, the Edinburgh publisher, bought the property in 1892 and introduced rhododendrons, azaleas and Japanese maples and bushes of berberis, which colour so beautifully in the autumn.

The woodland garden was begun in the 1950s, when R. ponticum was cleared to give space for many plants, including shrubs from the southern hemisphere and other parts of the world. Embothriums now reach the height of the oaks, which are indigenous to Argyll, and Crinodendron hookerianum, varieties of Clethra, Eucryphia and magnolias are amongst the 80 different varieties of deciduous trees which flourish in this natural setting. The primulas, irises, daffodils, narcissi and bluebells are a special feature in the spring and early summer. In 1990 a garden extension to the east of the house, near the point above Loch Etive, was begun and beyond it an old pond has been dredged and surrounded with trees. The house is not open to the public and at the time of writing (May 2013), the gardens will shortly be open to the public on Saturdays only.

## The Angus Garden, Barguillean

The road to Glen Lonan, which leaves the A85 just east of the Taynuilt Hotel, leads to an almost 'secret' garden created on the side of a hill. In 1956, a young reporter, Angus Macdonald, covering the troubles in Cyprus, was killed by a sniper's bullet. His parents, Neil and Betty Macdonald, created this garden in his memory. It stands at 450 feet above sea level on the south bank of an artificial loch, and because of its

Achnacloich House and gardens

The Angus Garden, Barguillean

exposed position, both Western hemlock (Tsuga heterophylla) and Corsican pine (Pinus nigra var. maritima) were planted to give shelter from the wind.

Within six years almost three hundred azaleas were brought from Exbury, most of which were massed round the edge of the loch, so that the glorious colours of the flowers, and of the autumn foliage, reflect in the water below. Later a pond was constructed, in what was formerly a bog, and many varieties of primula flourish in the damp soil. The garden, because of its seclusion, is a haven for wild birds, and swans are amongst the water fowl which constantly return to the loch. These are just some of the lovely gardens to be found both on the mainland and on the islands in Argyll. Many others also are open at selected times or can be viewed by appointment.

# CHAPTER 10: Argyll Today

## THE FORESTS

The first settlers of long ago might find it hard today to recognise the country they then knew. True, the landmarks, the great jagged peaks of the mountains, and the lochs and rivers remain, but the country itself is greatly changed, altered by the hand of man. Green sweeps of conifers now cover the hillsides. In 1909 the Crown Woodlands purchased the Inverliever Estate on the north shore of Loch Awe. The Forestry Commission was established in 1919 and the Crown Woodlands were transferred to it in 1926.

During the agricultural depression, between the two World Wars, land in the West Highlands remained very cheap. Whole hill farms were sold for forestry for as little as a pound an acre. The Forestry Commission is now the largest landowner in Argyll with around 160,000 hectares, of which 110,000 hectares have been planted. Nowadays ownership and management of Argyll's woodlands is divided almost equally between the Forestry Commission and the private sector.

Argyll is one of the main forest areas in the United Kingdom. It produces at least one million cubic metres (one sixth of the Scottish total) of timber a year for industry. This figure, which is rising as more forests mature, is likely to reach between 1.5 to 2.0 million cubic metres over the next 10 to 20 years. Eighty-five per cent of the trees being planted are sitka spruce, along with other conifers and, increasingly, some hardwoods. From its commencement, forestry was encouraged by government legislation. Dedication schemes were introduced in 1948 and again in the 1970s. Then, in 1980, following the introduction of Capital Transfer Tax, the Forestry Grant Scheme was initiated to replace existing acts. Private individuals and companies with large insurance schemes began buying large areas for planting trees on which tax avoidance was allowed.

The decade of the 1980s, however, saw an increase in national awareness of the effects of such mass planting of conifers on the environment. Foremost amongst the problems is the increased acidity of the soil. It is estimated that peat forms 15 per cent of most upland soils and that even in one short rotation of ploughing and tree planting irreversible desiccation can result. Also, according to scientists in Finland, afforestation can produce carbon monoxide in the atmosphere through the oxidisation of peat. Water is naturally affected and the burns, rivers and lochs, into which the forestry must drain, may be undergoing a metamorphosis, both from the use of fertilisers and from the acidity of the soil. Water supplies may be affected, as well as the water plants on which life exists, which in turn feed the aquatic creatures such as the native brown trout. All may be undergoing change. On the other side of the coin there are huge benefits to our climate in having extensive woodlands and it is estimated that Argyll's woods store 11 million tonnes of carbon and sequester an additional 0.6 million tonnes per annum.

The great benefit of deciduous trees, the leaves of which make humus and actually reduce the acidity of the soil, resulted in the introduction of the Broadleaved Woodland Grant Scheme in 1985. The government, pressurised by conservation bodies, such as the Countryside Commission for Scotland and the Nature Conservancy Council, and by the national press, removed forestry from the tax system in 1988. Since then a succession of new woodland support schemes, the Farm Woodland Scheme and new grants for native pinewoods have resulted in more mixed planting and renewed focus on Argyll's magnificent oak woodlands as well as ensuring that commercial conifer blocks are replanted after felling.

The Forestry Commission, following its great acquisition of land, built villages throughout Argyll, which rapidly became thriving communities with schools, and in most cases village halls. Sadly, thanks to economics, this is largely a thing of the past. Machinery has replaced manual labour, and of the forestry villages established, now only a few houses remain occupied by forestry workers. However, it is estimated that woodlands directly support 1,292 full-time equivalent jobs both within Argyll and beyond.

## FARMING

In the first decade of the 21st century the traditional livelihood of farming remained a major industry in Argyll. The outbreak of the Second World War in 1939 revitalised agriculture as grants and subsidies were given to stimulate vital food production. Following the war the Hill Farming Scheme of 1947 gave added impetus to farmers in upland areas. Money became available for improvement to farm houses and steadings and for fencing, draining, and regeneration of land.

Farming methods have since changed. Dairying is now confined mainly to Kintyre, Bute and Gigha. The closure of the creamery on Islay saw dairy farmers dispense with their milk-producing cows and change over within the space of a few months to beef production. Few hill farms today have even a house cow. Most carry cross-bred cattle, the calves being sold as stores. Fortunately the magnificent Highland cattle, descendants of the old stock which was once the mainstay of the economy, are now again in demand. Some are exported to Australia, America, and Europe, where, despite the difference in climate, they thrive in a new environment.

A new breed of cross Highland cattle officially registered as Luing has been raised by the Cadzow family on the island of Luing, off Easdale, south of Oban over the last 60 years. The black-faced sheep, which replaced so many cattle, are still predominant in Argyll. Cross ewes, which mate with breeds like Suffolk and Leicesters to produce bigger lambs, are increasing. Tractors have replaced farm horses. Corn

is now hardly grown and, since the very wet summer of 1985, most grass is made into silage and stored in large polythene bags.

As in other industries expenses have escalated. A shepherd's weekly wage, which in the 1950s was between £8 and £9, is now likely to be well over £300. Then, on his feet, he looked after 500 ewes. Today economics demand that, usually on a four-wheeled hill bike, he must herd at least 1,000 sheep.

Stock farming throughout Great Britain and the EU continues to benefit from various forms of financial support, without which the price of home-produced food would, of necessity, rise greatly in the shops. In Argyll farmers receive payments which reflect the difficulties of operating in a 'Less Favoured Area' and often to encourage them to farm in a way which supports the diverse natural habitats and huge range of native plant and animal species found on the west coast. Despite this, farmers in Argyll, as elsewhere in Scotland, find themselves faced with many difficulties. The cost of producing livestock continues steadily to rise, while prices, particularly in the sheep trade, can be very variable. Up until 2010, lambs, sold mainly as stores, did not fetch much more than they did in the mid-1980s. However, prospects for Scottish lambs and sheep are looking good at the start of the second decade of the 21st century thanks to world demand, particularly from Asia and the Far East, pushing up prices in the market.

Argyll farmers are resilient. The wolves and the cattle raiders of early times are now gone, but rain, gales and blizzards continue and life in the hills remains hard.

## FISH FARMING

Salmon farming, on a commercial scale, started in the 1970s. The industry in Argyll currently employs at least over 320 full-time staff on the farms, with many more being employed in processing, haulage and marketing. Salmon farming alone is considered to have injected £32 million into the Argyll and Bute economy in 2008 and produced almost 11,000 tonnes of fish for export.

Trout farming for the table, rather than restocking, began in the 1960s and there are now seven farms, four fresh and three saltwater sites, producing 1,400 tonnes out of a total Scottish production of approximately 3,000. The value of production at today's prices is roughly £2,310,000 per year.

The Crown Estates Commissioners have granted a considerable number of sea-bed leases to potential shellfish farmers. In the Argyll and Bute area there are over 30 businesses producing mainly mussels and Pacific oysters while experiments are being made with other species such as scallops. As with so many other industries, fish farming in the 21st century faces a number of challenges. The industry has grown faster than the market can stand, both at home and abroad, and its development as a whole has become controversial. Environmentalists protest about the visual impact of the fish cages, and there are issues relating to the impact of effluent on the sea bed. However, the industry is well regulated and is meeting these challenges.

Fish food is now much safer, most of the phosphorus and other potentially dangerous ingredients having been removed from its formula, but it still remains under scrutiny.

Great anxiety is also felt about the threat to wild stocks of fish from the escapees from fish farms. Rainbow trout in this country do not apparently reproduce, but it has been proved irrefutably that farmed and wild salmon interbreed. This is thought to weaken the genetic pool of wild fish stocks, thus reducing their viability. Farmed salmon can also be a source of sea lice parasites, which are implicated in disrupting and harming migratory wild fish as they return to their native rivers.

The industry works very hard to ensure high levels of biosecurity but damage to fish cages, whether through storms, floods or vandalism, can result in escapes. There are some concerns about the sustainability of the industry and in particular the conversion rate of wild fish caught, to make fish meal, to harvested product.

Shellfish farming, in contrast, does not need artificial feeding, a fact which should give encouragement to those involved in its production. The industry employs over a hundred people in Argyll. There are localised visual and sea bed impacts from shellfish farming but the industry is probably capable of significant further expansion without serious environmental impacts.

At the time of writing the Scottish aquaculture industry is vigorously pursuing opportunities to expand, backed by the Scottish Government. It is an important employer and wealth creator in many remote west-coast communities, providing skilled and rewarding jobs. At a number of locations within Argyll, there are now more people employed on sea lochs at fish and shellfish farms, than on the traditional land-based farms producing sheep and cattle. It does therefore make an outstanding impact on the economy of the West Highlands and the Isles.

## FISHING

In a county bordered by the sea and interlaced by sea lochs, fishing has been of great importance since time immemorial. In 2009 Oban had 129 vessels registered for fishing, 89 of which were under 10 metres long. The recorded landings at Oban in that year totaled 2,900 tonnes of shellfish with a value of £6.87 million. Campbeltown registered boats totalled 135, which included 83 boats less than 10 metres long. Over 500 people are employed as fishermen, almost wholly catching various species of shellfish, like prawns, lobsters and scallops. The shellfish catch weighed 5,600 tonnes and was valued at £11.37 million.

## RENEWABLE ENERGY

Currently the greatest change to the landscape must be made by the wind turbines, standing on high ground, the blades slowly turning against the horizon almost wherever one's eyes may roam. Renewable energy, whether by wind or water power in the many hydro-electric schemes currently under development, is certainly the greatest innovation of the present day.

## A CENTRE OF MUSIC AND THE ARTS

Perhaps it is the beauty of the country, the hills, the trees, the lochs and rivers and the surrounding seas, which has inspired so much music and art from the earliest times. The design and craftsmanship of the 8th-century crosses on the islands of Iona and Islay prove the skill of the masons who worked away so patiently with their primitive compasses and tools.

Tourism, in itself a major industry, has also provided an incentive to artists, sculptors, potters and jewellers, who find an outlet for their work in the craft shops and in the exhibitions which art societies arrange.

The haunting Hebridean chants, inspired by the love of a country which so many had to leave, are the themes of much of the Celtic music which is making a revival today. Oban alone has a Fiddle Club, a Bach Choir and an Operatic Society. Everywhere throughout Argyll and the Islands dramatic societies and musical groups enliven the long winter evenings in the same way that their ancestors held ceilidhs around the peat fires.

Gaelic, so long considered a dead language, is making a revival and is taught, often by travelling teachers, in many schools. The language has become more familiar thanks to wireless and television which bring us the Gaelic choirs and other singers at the Mod.

Classical dancing has also been introduced by Ballet West, a company founded near Taynuilt. Some schoolchildren learn ballet dancing and Highland dancing is increasingly popular – who does not love to see the those small kilted figures whirling round to the skirl of the pipes at the Highland Games?

The Highland Games, founded on old tradition, draw people from all over the world. Competitions like tossing the caber and throwing the hammer proved the strength of warriors to both friend and foe. Shinty, a game akin to hockey, is also an ancient sport. Many towns and villages have their own teams.

In contrast to age-old practices the film industry is an innovation of the present day. Much of *Rob Roy*, a big box-office draw, was made in Glencoe, where local Highland ponies and an army of extras gave an authentic touch.

Authors, like other creative people, find inspiration in much relating to the past. Many, at the same time, face the challenge of what lies ahead, for here the modern world inextricably invades the old.

Oban has its own radio station, Oban FM. Three of the main newspapers, the *Oban Times*, the *Argyllshire Advertiser* ('The Squeak') and the *Campbeltown Courier* are owned by a family concern; they have an international circulation to expatriates in Canada and Australia. Cowal has its own paper, the *Dunoon Observer & Argyllshire Standard*.

Thus has this part of Scotland, ignored by the Romans and considered, prior to the advent of road-building in the 18th century, a savage wilderness where only the most intrepid dared to tread, moved into the modern age.

It is now so easy to come to Argyll, by land, by sea, by air.

# Bibliography

Acts of Parliament, Scotland (A.P.S.) HM Register House, Edinburgh

Anderson, A.O. and M.O. (Eds) *Adamnan's Life of St Columba*, London & Edinburgh 1961

Anon, *Historical Account of the Clan Ranald*, Edinburgh 1849

Atholl & Tullibardine Families, Chronicles of, Vol. 1

Baillie, R. Letters & Journals, 3 Vols. Bannatyne Club 1841–42. Vol. III

Balfour-Melville, *James I, King of Scots*, Methuen & Co, London 1936

Barons of Phantisland, History of Clan MacCorquodale

Barnard, Alfred, *The Whisky Distilleries of the United Kingdom*. First published 1887 by *Harpers Weekly Gazette*. Reprinted David & Charles Publishers Ltd, 1969

Barrow, Professor G.W.S., *Robert the Bruce & the Community of the Realm of Scotland*, 1965

Black, R. 'Coll Ciotach', Gaelic Society of Inverness, XIVIII (1972–4)

Brown, A., *Memorials of Argyll*, Greenock 1889

Brown, P. Hume, *History of Scotland*, Cambridge 1900

Campbell, Lord Archibald, Records of Argyll, Edinburgh 1885

Campbell, Marion, *Argyll the Enduring Heartland*, Gateway Books, Bath 1977

Clan Ranald, (The) Anonymous Account of Edinburgh 1819

Cobbet, W., *State Trials*, 1810

Daiches, David, *Charles Edward Stuart*, Thames & Hudson, London 1983

Denmylne Mss. Ed. J.R. N. MacPhail.

Donaldson, Professor Gordon, *The Edinburgh History of Scotland* Vol 3, Mercat Press 1987

Donaldson, Professor Gordon, *Scottish Kings*, B.T. Batsford Ltd, London 1967

Duncan, A.A.M., *Scotland: the Making of the Kingdom The Edinburgh History of Scotland* Vol. I, Oliver & Boyd 1975

Exchequer Rolls of Scotland (E.R.) III, IV, XVI, XLV, H.M. Register House, Edinburgh.

Edmonstone, Sir Archibald, *Family History of Edmonstones of Duntreath*, Privately printed, Edinburgh 1875

Fergusson, Sir James of Kilerran, *Argyll in the Forty-Five*, Faber & Faber 1951

Fergusson, W., *The Edinburgh History of Scotland* Vol. 4, Oliver & Boyd 1987

Gaskell, Philip, *Morvern Transformed*, Cambridge University Press 1948

Gillies, Rev. W.A., *In Famed Breadalbane*, Clunie Press, Strathtay, Perthshire 1938

Glasgow Historical Society, House of Argyll & Clan Campbell

Gordon, Patrick of Ruthven, *A Short Abridgement of Britaine's Distemper*, Spalding Club 1844

Gordon, Seton, *Highways & Byways in the West Highlands*, MacMillan & Co Ltd, 1949

Grant, Doctor I.F., *Highland Folkways*, Routledge & Kegan Paul, London 1961

Grant, Doctor I.F., *The Lordship of the Isles*, Edinburgh 1935

Grant, Doctor I.F., *Social & Economic Development of Scotland Before 1603*, Edinburgh 1930

Grant, Doctor I.F., *Myth, Tradition & Story from Western Argyll*, Oban Times 1925

Gregory, D. *History of the Western Highlands & Isles to 1625*, 1836 (Reprinted 1975)

Gruamach, Donald, *The House of Islay*, 1962

Hamilton, H. *An Economic History of Scotland in the 18th Century*

Highland Tales, Misc. Vol. 1

Hill, G. *An Historical Account of the MacDonalds of Antrim*, Belfast 1873

*History of Wars in Ireland*, by a British officer

Johnston, C.H. & Campbell, K.M., *Connell on the Agricultural Holdings (Scotland) Acts*, 6th edition

Lamont, N. *Inventory of Lamont Papers*, Scottish National Record Society, 1914

Loder, J de V. *Colonsay & Oronsay in the Isles of Argyll*, Ed. 1935

MacDonald, A.J. & A.M. *The Clan Donald*, Inverness 1896–1904

MacDonald of Castleton, *Clan Donald*, MacDonald Publishers 1978

MacKechnie, Donald, *Inveraray Notes*, printed *Oban Times* 1986

McKechnie, Hector, *The Clan Lamont*, Lamont Society Edinburgh 1938

Mackechnie, John (Ed.), *The Dewar Manuscripts* Vol. 1, Glasgow 1963

MacGregor, A.G.M., *History of Clan Gregor*, Wm Brown Edinburgh 1898

McKerral, A. *Kintyre in the 17th Century* Edinburgh 1948

Mackie, J.D. *A History of Scotland*, Penguin Books 1964

MacPhail, J.R.N. (ed.) Extracts from the Collection of State Papaers in the Advocates Library known as the Denmyline Mass, S.H.S. 1920

MacPhail, J.R.N. (ed.) Highland Papers Vols I–IV, Edinburgh 1914–34

Martin, A. *Kintyre Country Life*, John Donald Publishers Ltd, Edinburgh 1987

Murray, W.H. *The West Highlands of Scotland*, Collins, London 1968

Murray, W.H. *The Islands of Western Scotland*, Eyre Methuen, London 1973

Napier, M. *The Memoirs of the Marquess of Montrose*, Edinburgh 1856

Nicholson, R. *The Edinburgh History of Scotland* Vol. 2

North of Scotland Hydro-Electric Board, 'Publications of Hydro Schemes in Argyll', Edinburgh

Orr, Willie, *Discovering Argyll, Mull & Iona*, John Donald Publishers Ltd. Edinburgh 1990

Pitcairns Criminal Trials III

Register of the Privy Council of Scotland, 3 Series, 38 Vols. Edinburgh 1877–1970

The Royal Commission on the Ancient & Historical Monuments of Scotland (RCAHMS) Vols 1–7, printed H.M. Stationery Office, Glasgow 1972–1992

Simpson, W. Douglas, *The Historical St Columba*, Oliver & Boyd, Edinburgh & London 1927

Skene, W.F. *Celtic Scotland*, 1886–90

Smith, Roger, 'Lochs and Locks along the beautiful Crinan Canal', Article in *Oban Times*, 1989

Smout, F.C. *A History of the Scottish People 1560–1830*, Collins, London 1960

Starforth, Michael, *An Official Short History of the Clan MacDougal*

The First Statistical Account of Scotland, 1791–99 (Ed. Sir John Sinclair) Vol. VIII, Argyll Mainland, reprinted E.P. Publishing Company 1983

New (2nd) Statistical Account, 1845, Wm Blackwood & Sons Edinburgh & London

Steel, Tom, *Scotland's Story*, Collins 1984

Steer. K.A. and Bannerman J.W.M., *Late Medieval Monumental Sculpture in the West Highlands*, RCAHMS, Edinburgh 1977

Stevenson, D. *Alasdair MacColla and the Highland Problem in the 17th Century*, John Donald Publishers Ltd 1980

Storie, Margaret C. *Islay – Biography of an Island*, Oa Press 1981

Turner, General James, *Memoirs of his own life & times*, Bannatyne Club 1827

*Victoria in the Highlands, the Personal Journal of Her Majesty Queen Victoria* (Ed. David Duff), Taplinger Publishing Co., New York 1969

Willcock, J. *The Great Marquess: Life & Times of Archibald, 8th Earl & 1st (and only) Marquess of Argyll*, Edinburgh & London 1903

Willcock, J. *A Scots Earl in Covenanting Times, being the life & times of Archibald 9th Earl of Argyll*, Edinburgh 1907

Wordsworth, Dorothy, *Recollections of a Tour Made in Scotland in 1803*, reprinted James Thin, The Mercat Press, Edinburgh 1981

# Notes

1. Corrie: a hollow in a hillside.
2. Peat: a brownish deposit of partially decomposed vegetable matter saturated with water found in temperate and cold regions, uplands and bogs, used as a fuel when dried and also as a fertiliser.
3. 'Sacred Stones', p. 43.
4. See Defeat of King Haakon of Norway, p. 26.
5. The Earldom of Menteith lay between the Rivers Teith and Forth.
6. See Devastation of Argyll by Alasdair MacColla 1645–47, p. 71.
7. See The End of the Lordship of the Isles, p. 41.
8. See Summary of Main Events 1513–1545, p. 59.
9. See Invasion of Alasdair MacColla MacDonald 1644, p. 69.
10. See Summary of Main Events 1329–1411 – The Lordship of the Isles, p. 60.
11. See The Treaty of Ardtornish, p. 41.
12. See Duart Castle, p. 73.
13. See James IV in Argyll, p. 59.
14. See Monmouth's Rebellion 1685, p. 75.
15. See The Rise of Clan Campbell, p. 29.
16. See p. 60.
17. See The Pass of Brander, p. 34.
18. See Defeat of Alasdair MacColla MacDonald 1647, p. 72.
19. See The Rising of 1745, p. 80.
20. This was the famous occasion, when asked to dine on a warship, they found themselves taken prisoner.
21. See Island of Coll, p. 26.
22. mark: a former monetary unit worth two-thirds of a pound.
23. See *Edinburgh History of Scotland*. Vol. 1 pp. 580–82.
24. See Summary of Main Events 1513–1545, Rebellion of Donald Dubh, p. 59.
25. See Defeat of Alasdair MacColla MacDonald 1647, p. 72.
26. See *A History of Clan Campbell Vol. 1* by Alastair Campbell of Airds, p. xxx.
27. See Glenstrae: The Landless MacGregors, p. 61.
28. RCAHMS Vol. 2 Lorn, p. 179.
29. Black Book of Taymouth (Records of Campbells of Glenorchy) pp. 35–6.
30. See The Cathedral of St Moluag, Lismore, p. 46.
31. The Exchequer Rolls: the Records of the expenditure of the Scottish Treasury, stored in Her Majesty's Register House, Edinburgh.
32. See Innis Chonnell Castle, p. 29.
33. For further information on West Highland sculpture see *The Royal Commission of the Ancient and Historical Monuments of Scotland (RCAHMS) Argyll Vols. 1–5 & 7*. Also Ster, K.A. and Bammerman, J.W.N. *Late Medieval Monumental Sculpture in the West Highlands* (Both published by H.M. Stationery Office).
34. See McGrigor, M. *Paths of the Pilgrims & Lives of the Early Saints*, p. 86.
35. RCAHMS Vol. 2. P. 295.
36. The Countess of Argyll's eldest daughter by her first marriage became the Countess of Moray in her own right and the title passed to her husband, *The Master of Doune,* on their marriage.
37. Hagbut is another name for arquebus.
38. Knipoch (present spelling) is now a hotel. A fragment of the older house is now all that remains.
39. Boot is a kind of rack in which nails were driven into the leg as it was tightened.
40. Gregory, History of the West Highlands and Isles, p. 386.
41. See Mingary Castle, Ardnamurchan, p. 16.
42. The now ruined village above Dalmally railway station can be reached by a footpath from the road leading to Duncan ban MacIntyre's Monument (map reference 162270 NNN12 NE).
43. A dirk is a small dagger, today largely ornamental, often worn in the top of a stocking.
44. See The Castles of Cowal: Toward Castle, p. 19.
45. See Stevenson, D. *Alasdair MacColla MacDonald & The Highland Problem in the 17th Century,* chapter 9.
46. See Craignish Castle, p. 31.
47. See Stevenson, D. *Alasdair MacColla MacDonald & The Highland Problem in the 17th Century,* pp. 235–6.
48. Stevenson, p. 237.
49. See RCAHMS Vol. 7 pp. 225–6.
50. See Campbell, Alastair, *A History of Clan Campbell.* Vol. 3, p. 189.
51. RCAHMS Vol. 2, p. 259.